**ASPATORE
BOOKS**

About Aspatore Books
Business Intelligence From Industry Insiders
www.Aspatore.com

Aspatore Books publishes only the biggest names in the business world, including C-level (CEO, CTO, CFO, COO, CMO, Partner) leaders from over half the world's 500 largest companies and other leading executives. Aspatore Books publishes the Inside the Minds, Bigwig Briefs, ExecEnablers and Aspatore Business Review imprints in addition to other best selling business books and journals. By focusing on publishing only the biggest name executives, Aspatore Books provides readers with proven business intelligence from industry insiders, rather than relying on the knowledge of unknown authors and analysts. Aspatore Books focuses on publishing traditional print books, while our portfolio company, Big Brand Books focuses on developing areas within the book-publishing world. Aspatore Books is committed to providing our readers, authors, bookstores, distributors and customers with the highest quality books, book related services, and publishing execution available anywhere in the world.

The *Inside the Minds* Series
Real World Intelligence From Industry Insiders
www.InsideTheMinds.com

Inside the Minds was conceived in order to give readers actual insights into the leading minds of business executives worldwide. Because so few books or other publications are actually written by executives in industry, *Inside the Minds* presents an unprecedented look at various industries and professions never before available. Each chapter is comparable to a white paper and is a very future oriented look at where their industry/profession is heading. In addition, the *Inside the Minds* web site makes the reading experience interactive by enabling readers to post messages and interact with each other, become a reviewer for upcoming books, read expanded comments on the topics covered and nominate individuals for upcoming books. The *Inside the Minds* series is revolutionizing the business book market by publishing an unparalleled group of executives and providing an unprecedented introspective look into the leading minds of the business world.

About Big Brand Books

Big Brand Books assists leading companies and select individuals with book writing, publisher negotiations, book publishing, book sponsorship, worldwide book promotion and generating a new revenue stream from publishing. Services also include white paper, briefing, research report, bulletin, newsletter and article writing, editing, marketing and distribution. The goal of Big Brand Books is to help our clients capture the attention of prospective customers, retain loyal clients and penetrate new target markets by sharing valuable information in publications and providing the highest quality content for readers worldwide. For more information please visit www.BigBrandBooks.com or email jonp@bigbrandbooks.com.

INSIDE THE MINDS:
The Art of Public Relations

Industry Visionaries Reveal the Secrets to Successful Public Relations

ASPATORE BOOKS

Published by Aspatore Books, Inc.
For information on bulk orders, sponsorship opportunities or any other questions please email store@aspatore.com. For corrections, company/title updates, comments or any other inquiries please email info@aspatore.com.

First Printing, 2002
10 9 8 7 6 5 4 3 2 1

ISBN 1-58762-063-4

Library of Congress Card Number: 2001119970

Cover design by Michael Lepera/Ariosto Graphics & Kara Yates

Material in this book is for educational purposes only. This book is sold with the understanding that neither any of the authors or the publisher is engaged in rendering legal, accounting, investment, or any other professional service.

This book is printed on acid free paper.

A special thanks to all the individuals that made this book possible.

Special thanks to: Jo Alice Hughes, Rinad Beidas, Kirsten Catanzano, Melissa Conradi, Molly Logan, Justin Hallberg

The views expressed by the individuals in this book do not necessarily reflect the views shared by the companies they are employed by (or the companies mentioned in this book). The companies referenced may not be the same company that the individual works for since the publishing of this book.

About Aspatore Business Reviews

The goal of Aspatore Business Reviews (Aspatore Business Review, Aspatore Technology Review, Aspatore Marketing Review, Aspatore Entrepreneurial Review) are to bring you the most important, condensed business intelligence from industry insiders on a range of different topics affecting every executive, expanding your breadth of knowledge and enabling you to innovate and outperform. Each journal focuses on specific issues affecting a particular profession/industry, written by leading C-Level executives (CEO, CFO, CTO, CMO, COO, Partner) currently in industry, rather than unknown writers, authors or research analysts who are absent from working in the current market environment. The Aspatore Business Review journals provide a distinct competitive advantage for our subscribers by featuring imperative business research from true industry insiders, with each issue featuring knowledge excerpts, white papers, articles, document analysis and other business intelligence. Aspatore Business Reviews focus on only the most pressing business issues in the most condensed format possible and are the best way to maintain your edge and keep current with your business reading in the most time efficient manner possible. Aspatore Business Reviews are interactive journals based on the submission of white papers, articles and knowledge excerpts from business leaders worldwide.

Each Aspatore Business Review follows the following special format, specifically designed by leading executives as the preferred way to comprehend business intelligence:

I. EXECUTIVE SUMMARY
The *Executive Summary* provides the highlight of the current journal, and enables you to very quickly scan the most important concepts.

II. ABR FEATURE
The *ABR Feature* focuses on a current topic affecting executives in every industry, from a variety of different C-Level (CEO, CFO, CTO, CFO, CMO, COO, Partner) perspectives.

III. IN THE KNOW
In the Know features knowledge excerpts from leading professionals on a variety of topics, enabling executives to expand their breadth of knowledge, communicate intelligently on a wide range of important issues, and develop ideas for innovation and new revenue opportunities within their own area of expertise.

IV. EXECUTIVE PERSPECTIVES
Executive Perspectives feature white papers on a variety of topics, submitted by C-Level (CEO, CFO, CTO, CMO, COO, Partner) executives from leading companies in major industries currently having a significant impact on the overall economy.

V. PROFESSION SPOTLIGHT
The *Profession Spotlight* focuses on a key C-Level (CEO, CFO, CTO, CFO, CMO, COO, Partner) or executive position, and the "Golden Rules" of that profession and other topics that will enable other types of executives to identify efficiencies, new product/service ideas, new revenue opportunities, interact better and implement innovative concepts into their own profession.

VI. INDUSTRY SPOTLIGHT
The *Industry Spotlight* section highlights a current industry, or part of an industry, that is affecting the majority of businesses in some way or another and provides opportunities for growth and new profit centers.

VII. IDEAS FOR INNOVATION
Ideas for Innovation features a series of question blocks that can be used as a starting point for an executive meeting, brainstorming session, or distributed to key managers as a way to stimulate new ideas.

ASPATORE MARKETING REVIEW
Tear Out This Page and Mail or Fax To:

Aspatore Books, PO Box 883, Bedford, MA 01730
Or Fax To (617) 249-1970

Name:

Email:

Shipping Address:

City: State: Zip:

Billing Address:

City: State: Zip:

Phone:

Lock in at the Current Rates Today-Rates Increase Every Year
Please Check the Desired Length Subscription:

1 Year ($1,090) _____   2 Years (Save 10%-$1,962) _____
5 Years (Save 20%-$4,360) _____   10 Years (Save 30%-$7,630) _____
Lifetime Subscription ($24,980) _____

(If mailing in a check you can skip this section but please read fine print below and sign below)
Credit Card Type (Visa & Mastercard & Amex):

Credit Card Number:

Expiration Date:

Signature:

Would you like us to automatically bill your credit card at the end of your
subscription so there is no discontinuity in service? (You can still cancel your
subscription at any point before the renewal date.) Please circle: Yes   No

***(Please note the billing address much match the address on file with your credit
card company exactly)**

Terms & Conditions
We shall send a confirmation receipt to your email address. If ordering from Massachusetts, please
add 5% sales tax on the order (not including shipping and handling). If ordering from outside of the
US, an additional $51.95 per year will be charged for shipping and handling costs. All issues are
paperback and will be shipped as soon as they become available. Sorry, no returns or refunds at any
point unless automatic billing is selected, at which point you may cancel at any time before your
subscription is renewed (no funds shall be returned however for the period currently subscribed to).
Issues that are not already published will be shipped upon publication date. Publication dates are
subject to delay-please allow 1-2 weeks for delivery of first issue. If a new issue is not coming out for
another month, the issue from the previous quarter will be sent for the first issue. For the most up to
date information on publication dates and availability please visit www.Aspatore.com.

INSIDE THE MINDS:
The Art of Public Relations

Industry Visionaries Reveal the Secrets to Successful Public Relations

CONTENTS

Christopher P.A. Komisarjevsky　　11
WINNING COMMUNICATIONS FOR TOMORROW'S LEADERS: THE TOOLS AND TECHNIQUES FOR SUCCESS

Rich Jernstedt　　59
THE CREATION OF TRUST

Don Middleberg　　85
THE NEW BREED OF THE INFORMED, PROACTIVE CONSUMER: THE PROSUMER

Ron Watt, Sr.　　109
PUBLIC RELATIONS AS AN ART AND A CRAFT

Richard Edelman　　125
THE POWER OF PUBLIC RELATIONS IN A COMPLEX WORLD

Lou Rena Hammond   **143**
SUCCESS IN PUBLIC RELATIONS

Anthony J. Russo, Ph.D.   **153**
THE ART AND SCIENCE OF
PUBLIC RELATIONS

Thomas L. Amberg   **171**
CRITICAL ELEMENTS OF SUCCESS
IN PUBLIC RELATIONS

Robyn M. Sachs   **193**
SMALL BUSINESS BANG! DESIGNING AND
LAUNCHING A SUCCESSFUL SMALL
BUSINESS PR CAMPAIGN

Patrice A. Tanaka   **227**
PR: A KEY DRIVER OF BRAND MARKETING

David Finn   **243**
AN ESSENTIAL FUNCTION IN A
DEMOCRATIC SOCIETY

WINNING COMMUNICATIONS FOR TOMORROW'S LEADERS: THE TOOLS AND TECHNIQUES FOR SUCCESS

CHRISTOPHER P.A. KOMISARJEVSKY
Burson-Marsteller Worldwide
President and
Chief Executive Officer

The CEO as Chief Communications Officer

An important challenge for the public relations industry is helping people understand that a company's chief executive is actually the company's chief communications officer. No one else in the company has the responsibility the chief executive has; no one has the platform the chief executive holds; and most importantly, no one has the understanding of the goals and ultimate vision of the company like the chief executive.

From the public's perspective, the chief executive symbolizes the company, speaks for the company, and is seen as possessing the company's brand values. A strong CEO – delivering the right messages – makes an enormous difference in the valuation of a company, while inaction or missteps can have dire, instantaneous consequences.

We recommend that CEOs take the following steps to maximize their effectiveness:

Set an agenda and create a vision for the future; then become the architect of the company's vision and values. If successful, they will be better able to recruit and retain the best talent that they need to execute their agenda and gain respect nationally and internationally.

Build a strong senior management team, and keep team members acting in unison.

Measure – and manage – what matters: quality service and products, the level of stock recommendations, and "best-in-class" and "employer-of-choice" status.

Listen carefully to word of mouth and online activity – about their company and about themselves.

Communicate regularly and proactively with internal and external audiences, using all appropriate channels and methods of communication.

Listen to customers, clients, employees, financial community members, and shareholders, so that they meet expectations.

Know the type of information that shareholders need, and deliver it personally.

Keep pace with change, and use technology to their competitive advantage, so they can operate on a global scale, accelerate change and decision-making, and be recognized as forward-thinking, innovative leaders.

At a *Chief Executive* magazine CEO roundtable, Dana Mead of Tenneco asked other CEOs, "How many of you have talked to institutional investors about your company, spending time on leadership development, employee training or environmental performance?" Not many had, as it turned out. CEOs who make the time to communicate with stakeholders can gain a competitive advantage; those who do not run the risk of letting others manage their fate.

The chief executive's visibility and ability to articulate his or her company's unique niche in the market are essential to shaping public perception. When people look at a company and to the chief executive, they look at the chief executive's values, and then they wait to see if those values and beliefs are reflected in production processes, employee treatment, customer relations, and other company operations and practices.

Public relations professionals are responsible for using communications to encourage a company to perform in a manner consistent with its mission and values. Public relations is, therefore, not only a matter of communication, but also a matter of behavior.

Communications Capital™

All business professionals know that the value of a corporation is built upon tangible assets – plants and machinery – and intangible assets, or its intellectual capital. In fact, in tomorrow's business environment, intangible assets will grow significantly in importance. Although opinions differ on how to categorize intangibles, we divide them into four categories:

- *Market Capital:* The intelligence that goes i和 and developing new products and servic physical product itself. It also includes intangible attributes closely related to products, such as trademarks, patents, brand reputation, corporate reputation, and other marketing materials.
- *Human Capital:* The knowledge, skills, and competencies that managers and employees possess.
- *Structural Capital:* Any type of knowledge or innovation that has an impact on IT platforms, internal processes, manufacturing, or distribution.
- *Relationship Capital:* The company's relationships with its customers and other stakeholders, including investors, government agencies, and communities.

Historically, the value of intangibles was considered relatively modest compared with financial assets, such as buildings, equipment, and inventory. But we now know that this is not the case.

Forbes ASAP put it best: "Today, when intangible assets can make up a huge portion of a company's value, and when that value is remeasured every business day by stock market analysts and traders, our current system of financial measurement has become increasingly disconnected from what appears to be truly valuable in the new economy." It is estimated today that intangible assets are three times greater in value than tangible assets. For example, Microsoft has very little in the way of tangible assets, but it is greatly respected by the entire marketplace for its intangible assets and intellectual capital.

To quote Leif Edvinsson of Scandia Insurance, whom many consider to be "the father of intellectual capital," "The intellectual capital of nations is the new wealth of nations."

Communications Capital is the strategic use of communications to leverage a company's intellectual capital, and as a result gain even more value – higher valuations – than might otherwise have been possible. It encompasses the proper review, assessment, packaging, and communication of intangible assets, and can mean the difference between success and failure. At our firm, we believe Communications Capital is a Fifth Capital – an intangible asset category that infuses the other four (Market, Human, Structural, and Relationship Capital) and enables them to resonate in the marketplace.

On the upside, the benefits of Communications Capital, of leveraging and communicating intangibles, are wide-ranging:

❑ Positive analyst recommendations
❑ Increased investor demand
❑ A higher number of repeat customers
❑ Premium pricing
❑ A larger number of committed employees

❑ A broader talent pool
❑ Motivated partners
❑ Higher quality vendors

Because these benefits contribute to a company's bottom line in a very real way, Communications Capital is easily redeemed for hard currency.

Our firm has begun to explore the impact of communications on influential business people – CEOs, senior executives, financial analysts, government officials' and journalists. Our results show companies that communicate their strategy command a higher MVA (market value added) and EVA (economic value added) than other firms. Investors are also more likely to put a higher value on the intangible assets of a firm that has effective communications.

Building Communications Capital is a key CEO responsibility. To perform his or her job to the fullest, CEOs need the best that communications can bring. Failing to accept this challenge can create precipitous gaps between a company's actual worth and its perceived value among key stakeholders. These gaps can seriously damage a company's reputation, making it less likely that audiences will invest in the company, purchase its products or services, or look upon it favorably as an employer or as a joint-venture or strategic-alliance partner.

We recommend a multi-step, integrated process for reviewing, assessing, packaging, and communicating intangible assets. Companies wishing to develop strong Communications Capital need to develop communications processes with the following features:

❏ *Right leadership:* Support from a company's top leadership. The CEO must be involved.
❏ *Right resources*: The capacity, infrastructure, and staff to deliver the correct amount of intangible information in a timely manner.
❏ *Right strategy:* An emphasis on the company's vision and strategy.
❏ *Right relationships:* The ability to develop a dialogue with key stakeholder groups and build relationships over time.
❏ *Right information:* Disclosure of relevant intangible-asset information with stakeholders in a straightforward manner.
❏ *Right feedback:* Shifting dialogue from one-way to two-way, always respecting different opinions and measuring progress on key communications goals.

Five Principles of Public Relations

Public relations can be broken down into the following five principles:

THE ART OF PUBLIC RELATIONS

1.   Proactive communication is a strategic business resource that helps shape the way people view a company by giving them the information they need to make an informed decision.

2.   Communications by themselves are empty; however, when they mirror behavior, they become effective – talk is cheap, but action counts at the end of the day. When the public looks at a company, it listens to the company's words and actions.

3. To deliver valuable results for the client, it is necessary to combine direct (advertising through the mail and the Internet) and indirect (communications that encourage third-party support) communications. To be effective in communications, there is no single way to send particular messages. Receivers differ in how they best assimilate information. Public relations professionals need to recommend the best channels for different audiences.

4. Public relations professionals have the responsibility to communicate in a well-considered, exciting, and interesting way, so messages distinguish themselves from the proliferation of communications. Strong public relations is thoughtful; it understands that individuals make decisions, which requires that the information be interesting, intelligent, and respectful.

5. Powerful, high-quality communications are built upon substantive information – knowledge, research, and creativity. Good public relations is not focused exclusively on good stories, and it never hides from the tough issues that need to be addressed. Rather, it deals with all facets of a company, including both difficult and easy issues.

Golden Rules of Public Relations

Listen carefully to clients, colleagues, media representatives, and other interested parties to understand all relevant viewpoints and perspectives. This approach enables public relations professionals to make judgments that address all appropriate issues, concerns and objectives.

Never lose sight of the relationship between words and deeds. Words alone are meaningless – they must rest upon a foundation of action. Public relations works only when words mirror behavior.

Approach every assignment with respect for the people who will make the ultimate judgment as to the worthiness of a product or service and the value of a company.

Follow the aged Italian proverb: "Deceit has short legs." It applies directly to public relations, in that no one can hide from the truth, and that people are able to distinguish between truth and falsity.

Understand and appreciate the chief executive's role, his or her influence, and the responsibility of communicating on a company's behalf.

Focus on integrated communications that combine different techniques – advertising, public relations, and direct marketing – that when taken together are effective in communicating a specific message to the target audience.

Win credibility among, and support of, internal and external audiences by communicating consistently. Companies make a serious mistake when they communicate regularly when times are good and abruptly stop when conditions take a turn for the worse.

Make research a high priority, and allocate the necessary resources to ensure the company achieves the most groundbreaking results. Research is one of your most direct paths to understanding clients and persuading a market.

View public relations proactively as a strategic resource that shapes opinions and builds a framework of informed opinions, so the public can make an informed decision based upon this framework.

The CEO Effect

Because a company's reputation is closely tied to the chief executive's reputation, the chief executive plays a critical role in shaping the company's reputation. As part of its ongoing research into the relationship between the chief executive's reputation and the company's reputation, our firm launched Building CEO Capital, a CEO reputation survey of 1,155 business influentials who fall within five key stakeholder groups in the United States: CEOs, senior executives, financial analysts/institutional investors, the business media, and government officials. The survey reveals that chief executives are evaluated by more than the bottom line.

In today's increasingly competitive marketplace, it comes as no surprise that the contribution of the chief executive's reputation to the corporate brand has increased to 48%. This estimate has grown 20% since our first CEO survey was conducted in1997. Also in the survey, credibility claimed the number-one position among factors driving CEO reputation, followed by high ethical standards and good internal communications. Increasing shareholder value, while an important component, is not among the top drivers of CEO favorability.

Drivers of CEO Reputation

❑ Is believable
❑ Demands high ethical standards
❑ Communicates clear vision inside company
❑ Attracts and retains quality management team
❑ Motivates and inspires employees
❑ Cares about customers
❑ Manages crises and downturns effectively
❑ Communicates clear vision outside company
❑ Increases shareholder wealth
❑ Executes well on strategic plan

Leveraging a CEO's reputation is a powerful tool that delivers tangible payoffs, particularly with respect to its impact on stock price. Almost all stakeholders report that CEO reputation influences their decisions to:

❑ Purchase stock in a company (95 percent)
❑ Believe a company if under pressure from the media (94 percent)
❑ Recommend a company as a good alliance or merger partner (93 percent)
❑ Maintain confidence in company when share price is lagging (92 percent)

An impressive 88 percent are likely to recommend a company as a good place to work if the CEO has the right stuff. Clearly, a strong CEO makes an enormous difference in the valuation of a company and its ability to attract financial and human capital.

Other findings include the following:

Pleasing and meeting the expectations of stakeholders place undue pressure on CEOs. The time period they are given to perform favorably is shortening, and their failure rate is skyrocketing. Stakeholders report that CEOs can survive, on average, only five poor earnings quarters before their jobs are in jeopardy.

By far, print – major business magazines, followed closely by national newspapers – is the leading source of information on CEOs for all audiences. Trade-specific publications are another commonly used source of information on the activity occurring in the corner office or cubicle. As business continues to be top-of-mind for key stakeholders, word of mouth also remains a powerful source of CEO-related news and information. Other, less-often used sources of CEO news include television, investor meetings and reports, advertising, and the Internet.

The Internet – Web sites, company home pages, and chat rooms – continues to rise as an important resource for information on CEOs. Since 1997, Internet usage has grown a remarkable 340 percent. Also, members of the media are frequent visitors to company Web sites for CEO-related information.

Our CEO reputation research extends beyond the United States. Research has been conducted in the United Kingdom, Australia, and Germany. We found that CEO reputation matters the world over:

❏ Opinion-makers in the United Kingdom report CEO reputation accounts for 49 percent of a company's reputation.
❏ Among Australian financial analysts and members of the business media, CEO reputation is responsible for 52 percent of a company's reputation.
❏ In Germany, Burson-Marsteller and *Wirtschaftswoche* magazine – Germany's equivalent to *Business Week* – asked executives to estimate the extent to which a corporate reputation is attributable to the CEO. German executives responded with a staggering estimate of 64 percent.

The importance of CEO reputation is inherent in *Fortune* magazine's "Most Admired Companies Study." It is also the basis of *Worth* magazine's annual "Top 50 CEOs" issue, which specifically looks at reputation as a determining factor in the value of a company's stock price.

CEOs and Technology

But there is yet another challenge to building CEO reputation and shareholder value, and it goes to the heart of how people communicate today and in the future. This challenge is technology.

Our firm teamed with the marketing group of *Fortune* in 2000 to study what was "on the minds of CEOs." As part of our On the Minds of CEOs study, we spoke with 707 new-economy and traditional-economy CEOs from around the world to find out how they viewed their leadership responsibilities in the 21st century and how technology was affecting their jobs. The results are dramatic. Here's what the findings revealed about the CEOs who participated in the survey:

❏ A staggering 91 percent reported logging on to the Internet.

❏ CEOs spend an average of six hours per week online.

❏ In the six-month period preceding the survey, 96 percent of the CEOs worldwide had exchanged e-mail; 94 percent had visited online news and information sources; 87 percent spent time on their own Web sites; and 75 percent monitored the Web sites of their competition.

❏ Nearly six out of every ten CEOs are using the Internet once or more per day to check their company's share price. This finding is not surprising, considering how many CEOs – and boards of directors – view share price as a performance review.

❏ Comparatively few CEOs have participated in online chats. However, the signals are strong that this will soon change.

❏ While there is a surge in CEO usage of online resources, the majority of CEOs continue to rank traditional media – such as magazines and newspapers – along with the advice of their technology staffs, as being more critical when making technology decisions.

❏ The vast majority of the CEOs (83 percent) report having an Internet strategy for their company. CEOs increasingly understand that the Internet is no longer a novelty, and they appoint themselves as evangelists and engineers of their company's e-business platforms.

❏ When discussing their own goals for their companies, CEOs focus squarely on the competition for talent, reporting that people assets are the number-one concern that keeps them up at night.

❏ When it comes to corporate growth, CEOs are focused on achieving superior financial results and on being perceived as the industry leader and as having a strong focus on delivering value to customers. To accomplish this, CEOs believe strong internal communications, high ethical standards, and strong corporate governance are key.

On balance, these CEOs focus on a vision, on understanding and harnessing the power of new technology, and on meeting expectations. To quote a prediction from Lou Gerstner, CEO of IBM: "…the real storm was going to come when the world's established enterprises came to the Net."

The Power of Online Influencers

The Internet is a forum where anyone can speak freely and share an opinion in an uncontrolled environment, unlike traditional media that always have filters – a reporter, a researcher, or a broadcaster who reviews the information and presents a reasoned opinion. Public relations professionals need to understand how to influence the pure, unfiltered opinions that are shared over the Internet to reach their own goals, as well as the goals of their clients. To accomplish this, public relations professionals need to first identify the influential people who shape public opinion online and offline and who share the uncanny ability to seamlessly spread information by word-of-mouth.

Our firm broke new ground by collaborating with RoperASW in research into the group of influential movers and shakers who have mastered these virtual relationships and communications channels. We have identified this powerful new group of opinion leaders who exert such a strong impact on online and offline content and commerce as e-fluentials[SM] and they occupy key positions in their companies' future success.

In the old economy – or the offline world – one person was generally thought to have an impact on the attitudes and behavior of approximately two people. Today, an e-fluential has an impact on the attitudes and behavior of approximately 14 people. The challenge today, and in the future, will be for companies to understand e-fluentials and harness their potential impact to achieve measurable business results.

The classic 1970s Faberge Organics shampoo television commercial serves as a dramatic example of how the opinions of e-fluentials travel across cyberspace. In the commercial, a woman tells two friends about the product, and they tell two friends and so on and so on, and as she speaks, her image multiplies across the screen. If that commercial were broadcast today and that woman was an e-fluential, she would influence 14 friends, with her opinion spreading in multiples of 14 rather than two.

E-fluentials, who comprise 10 percent (11.1 million) of the U.S. online adult population – up from 8 percent (9 million) since Burson-Marsteller's first study in 1999 – were among the first to explore the Internet frontier and remain today's most prominent online trailblazers.

E-fluentials' characteristics include the following:

- ❏ *Marketing Multipliers:* Have opinions that are far-reaching and radiate to a level of influence disproportionate to their actual size.
- ❏ *Influentials:* Extend their influence beyond the online world – they have a say in the purchasing decisions (online and offline) of approximately 155 million consumers, and their families and peers regularly approach them for information, opinions, and advice.
- ❏ *Avid Communicators:* Communicate with more people online – far more active users of e-mail, newsgroups, bulletin boards, listservs, and other online vehicles when conveying their messages.
- ❏ *Information Sponges:* Absorb more information than general Internet users and glean it from a more diverse array of sources.
- ❏ *Technology Savvy:* Are Internet experts – they go online on a daily basis, while 66 percent spend at least two hours online per day.
- ❏ *New Product Innovators:* Are inclined toward innovations and new technologies, and this holds true for their buying patterns.
- ❏ *Civic-minded:* Are more likely to vote, attend public meetings, serve on local committees, and make speeches.

The following are the Six Secrets of E-fluentials, which were uncovered by our latest research:

Secret #1: E-fluentials are infectious.

E-fluentials make waves. They project their opinions far beyond the scope of their individual contacts. An e-fluential imparts an experience to 14 individuals on average. The vast majority spreads the word through multiple communication channels. These electronic town criers are as likely to share information on products and services offline as they are to relay their experiences online.

Because of the extensive reach of e-fluentials' opinions, it is critical that companies establish brand recognition and win customer preference among these opinion-brokers to expand their customer base.

Secret #2: E -fluentials share negative experiences.

E-fluentials spread news describing a negative experience to a wider audience than they would a positive experience. For example, while e-fluentials pass along positive experiences to 11 people on average, they warn 17 people about negative experiences – reverberating to 55 percent more people than their endorsements. Since e-fluentials highly value one-on-one dialogue and information exchange, companies can better manage their reputations by inviting feedback and providing a forum where e-fluentials can chat about their positive and negative experiences – and query others.

Secret #3: Gender affects e-fluentials' choice of information sites.

When developing customer acquisition and retention campaigns, marketers need to be aware of different categories of e-fluentials. Male and female e-fluentials go online to provide or read opinions with diverging agendas.

While men seek opinions and provide advice on technology, women e-fluentials primarily search for information pertaining to food and health, and they mobilize others on women's issues. By knowing where specific types of e-fluentials surf online, marketers can more precisely personalize their campaigns and reap greater rewards from their messages, events, and cause-related programs.

Information-Seeking Differences by Gender

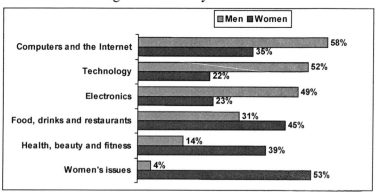

(Percent of e-fluentials likely to exchange opinions on opinion Web sites)

Secret #4: E-fluentials uncover the inside scoop.

E-fluentials do their homework before embarking on a new purchase. An astounding 84 percent of e-fluentials have read product- or service-related messages on opinion Web sites in the past year. Many e-fluentials use opinion sites such as Epinions.com, Amazon.com and Planetfeedback.com.

Regardless of how frequently they visit opinion Web sites, e-fluentials cannot be fooled by "opinions" posted by hired professionals. Nearly seven in ten e-fluentials report that if they question the legitimacy of an opinion, they will double-check the potentially questionable information with other offline or online sources (72 percent double-check offline, and 69 percent double-check online). Companies can ensure the accuracy of online information that rates the quality of their products or services by including on their sites links to other external sources that provide ratings.

E-fluentials' Responses to Potentially Biased Reviews on Opinion Web sites

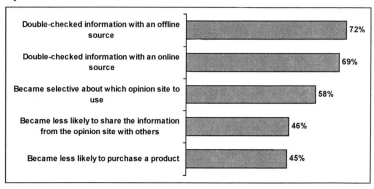

Secret #5: E-fluentials value company Web sites.

Company Web sites attract e-fluentials. Across a wide variety of sectors – technology, retail, finance, pharmaceutical, and automotive – company Web sites are the most widely used online information source of brand, product, and service information among e-fluentials.

E-fluentials are more likely to turn to company Web sites than to online magazines or opinion Web sites for industry information. Because e-fluentials can be categorized as "information sponges," companies need to develop a straightforward, easy-to-use information-retrieval system for the products and services featured on their Web sites.

Online Information Sources by Sector

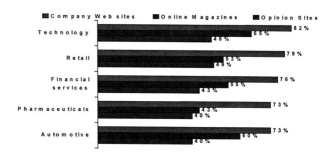

(Percent of e-fluentials who exchange opinions online about companies, brands, products, and services)

Secret #6: E-fluentials are ready to commit.

E-fluentials respond to direct e-mail campaigns. Although e-fluentials are critical of unsolicited e-mails – 94 percent have deleted them, and 72 percent have requested to be taken off a mailing list at one time or another – a significant group takes action.

A sizeable 90 percent of e-fluentials report that they read unsolicited e-mails from known sources they trust. A driving force behind e-fluentials' decision to open unsolicited e-mail is familiarity with the company brand. Because an admired brand name has the power to motivate e-fluentials to act positively, companies with favorable reputations will succeed in having their messages heard.

More than one-third (39 percent) of e-fluentials have visited a new Web site after opening an unsolicited e-mail. About one-fifth (21 percent) have subscribed to a newsletter or forwarded the e-mail to someone else. These findings reveal marketing dollars are better spent building trusted brands offline and online than aimlessly attracting visitors to Web sites.

Actions Ever Taken in Response to Unsolicited E-mail

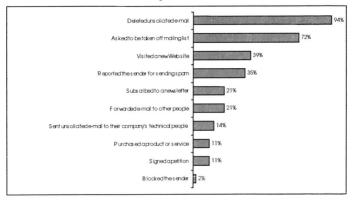

The far-reaching effect of this powerful group of men and women can make or break a brand, marshal or dissolve support for business and consumer issues, and provide insight into events as they unfold. For companies and marketers, there is an urgent need to earn e-fluentials' trust, approval, and support. E-fluentials' influence has been proved to run far and wide.

In this complex world, one must understand not only the direction of the traditional media, but also the shaping of public opinion. This must be done within the framework of knowing that information travels at the speed of light. Therefore, a global corporation looking to help shape the opinion of a company or to deal with a crisis has to understand that things happen instantaneously. Every piece of information has global consequences within seconds. Not only, then, does a public relations company have to deal with the traditional media, newspapers, television, radio, but also with the Internet and its implications.

A New Management Era

We have entered an era where professional relationships are being reexamined and redefined in new and exciting ways. The pace of change is constant and moving ahead at lightening speed. Ever-fluctuating economic conditions and the Internet have forever changed the dynamics of the employer-employee relationship. Companies that may have once taken for granted their market share, brand equity, and tangible and intangible assets – the most important of which is their employees – are now competing head-to-head with new rivals for market share and the best talent.

Customer, client, and employee expectations are rising to new levels, and in the process they are creating new work patterns, management styles, and ways to motivate employees.

We need to move now beyond the tried-and-true. It's time to rethink how we manage and lead people if we want to retain our best talent and mitigate the high cost of turnover. It appears as though the days of "chainsaw management" have passed, and a more nurturing, personal approach to management is what's needed.

In the book I wrote with my wife Reina – *Peanut Butter and Jelly Management: Tales from Parents, Lessons for Managers* – we apply the personal lessons we have learned from childrearing to management situations in the workplace. This new management approach serves as an alternative to traditional approaches, better positions a company to attract and retain the most talented, and mitigates high turnover costs, which can cost as much as 150 percent of the departing employee's salary.

Because good parenting and good management have much in common, being a strong manager requires many of the same skills and qualities associated with being a good parent. More often than not, if we carefully listen and watch children at home, consider their upbringing and our own, and learn from these experiences, we can become better managers and leaders.

Good leaders and good parents make a real effort to understand human nature and make a point of trying to relate personally to people. From my perspective, that means building people's self-esteem and trying to create a team culture so people can learn from each other, a culture that reflects their own values and sense of what's right.

Daniel Goleman, author of the acclaimed books *Emotional Intelligence* and *Working with Emotional Intelligence,* wrote a thoughtful article on this subject in *The Harvard Business Review.* In his article, "Leadership That Gets Results," he notes, "Like parenthood, leadership will never be an exact science. But neither should it be a complete mystery to those who practice it. In recent years, research has helped parents understand the genetic, psychological, and behavioral components that affect their 'job performance.' With our new research, leaders too can get a clearer picture of what it takes to lead effectively. And perhaps as important, they can see how they can make that happen."

From my perspective as a CEO and parent, I have learned that a number of parental experiences have direct parallels to workplace management strategies:

Understanding family members' different personalities, talents, and inclinations = Accepting diversity within the workforce

Practicing for Little League = Encouraging practice or rehearsal

Fiercely guarding the goal in street hockey = Keeping your cool during a crisis

Having the courage to dive into the deep end of the swimming pool = Trying something new and taking reasonable risks

Cleaning the garage together = Creating strong teams

Remaining calm during emergency-room visits = Being in control during a crisis

Calming an injured child = Building an emotional bond

Removing the training wheels from a bicycle = Having the courage to let go of the familiar and assume greater responsibility

My son Nicholas provided another example. One day at school, Nicholas decided to get into the garbage can and stomp around the classroom. His teacher told him not to do it and asked him why he wanted to stomp in the garbage can. Nicholas responded, "It's a free country isn't it?" As a result, Nicholas spent his lunch period outside the principal's office. After learning about the event at home, my wife and I decided Nicholas needed to write a letter of apology to his teacher. His action was disrespectful to the teacher and the class.

The lesson that applies to both Nicholas and the workplace is that we all make mistakes and do stupid things; however, when we act in this way we must acknowledge our actions and move on. In the business world, mistakes are not always acknowledged, and blame is often passed around.

Another personal-life lesson relates to the year I spent in the military as a helicopter pilot in Vietnam. This experience taught me what is important. Crisis situations force people to prioritize to decide how future behavior will support these gained priorities. They also allow people to take a step back and ask challenging questions regarding their values and goals.

Although business executives and parents can play similar roles, there are key differences. First, in business there are times when you have to make absolutely objective, very tough decisions. These must be completely devoid of emotion. I don't believe you find that in the family because you have such a strong, inherently emotional bond that exists between parents and children. The second major difference is that when you run a commercial enterprise, you have a very important responsibility to deliver growth and earnings. That becomes the driver of every decision you make. You don't find the same thing within a family.

There are also situations where peanut-butter-and-jelly management may not be right for a company: those situations when a company is facing radical change and when radical decisions need to be made. That doesn't mean the situation can't be addressed with a strong sense of values, mentoring, clarity, and explanation. But sometimes you need to act very quickly to turn around a company that's having a difficult time. What my wife and I are suggesting takes a lot of time. It's not quality time. It's time. Sometimes businesses don't have that time.

Does peanut butter and jelly management require managers to treat employees like children or assume a parental approach? Not at all. It does mean, though, that employees will benefit greatly from more personal involvement, care, attention, fair guidelines, flexibility, and understanding. It also means that this decade's successful corporate leaders will have to be people-focused and apply to the workplace the same strategies that work so well on the home front.

Here are ten behaviors that have a proven track record:

❑ Be a leader first and a manager second. Manage the way you would want to be managed.
❑ Be attentive, listen, and invite dialogue.
❑ Communicate, communicate, and then communicate some more. Keep in mind communication is a two-way street.
❑ Create strong values, and lead by action.

❑ Don't ask anyone to do anything you wouldn't do yourself.

❑ Learn to be flexible and patient.

❑ Create a team, know when to delegate, and provide the skills and tools necessary for team members to do their jobs well.

❑ Focus your energy on activities that are really important.

❑ Have confidence in yourself, and build it in others.

❑ Remember: You're on center stage – and everyone is watching.

No one, regardless of experience, has all the answers to every management challenge, and clearly the home is not where all the answers can be found. But since creating successful family relationships is one of the toughest jobs – if not the toughest job – on earth, the home is a good place to start.

Crisis Management

For a public relations company, handling a crisis situation boils down to a relationship between fact and emotion. The following guidelines can help public relations professionals when providing crisis communications services:

❑ Ensure that when the company decides to speak, it speaks with compassion and understanding.

❏ Keep communications focused and factual.
❏ Serve as a reliable and trusted source of information by keeping target audiences continuously informed of events in an organized manner. Communications need to properly focus people's intellect and emotions.
❏ Reassure all interested parties by providing enough factual information that listeners can develop an informed perspective on the situation. This goal can be difficult to accomplish because, generally, many facts are unavailable at the early stages of a crisis. Professionals should therefore make the best use of the facts at hand.
❏ Ensure that crisis counsel is informed by perspective and professional insight into the situation, regardless of the amount of available information.

The events of Tuesday, September 11, 2001, have changed the definition of leadership unalterably. As much as that tragic Tuesday is a political story of hatred among peoples, it is also a business story that tests how CEOs respond to the unexpected and the unimaginable. Never before have so many CEOs confronted a catastrophe of such proportions. Never before have so many CEOs been forced to face the raw emotions of so many grief-stricken employees and families.

Chief executives' behavior in the aftermath of a tragedy is critical to the recovery of employee productivity, loyalty, and ultimately their companies' reputation. The following guidelines should provide all leaders with best practices during times of crisis:

Be Visible. This is not a time for CEOs to be missing in action or huddled in executive committees for hours at a time. CEOs must leave their offices to connect with others during trying times. They must take to the halls, telephones, and electronic networks. The CEO's hyper-visibility provides much-needed reassurance to all interested parties.

Communicate Tirelessly. CEOs must take action following a crisis – hold employee meetings, and provide a toll-free number for employees working outside the office. These meetings should be held every day, and at the same time, throughout the crisis period. Use all channels of communications – e-mail, voice mail, and company intranet – to reach out to employees. Research has shown that during emergencies, organizations often restrict the flow of information and reduce the number of information channels.

Keep Communications Appropriate. CEOs should be extra cautious of everything they say or write during emergency situations. Language should always be appropriate and sensitive to the situation. In addition, CEOs should inform clients of the extent to which business may be compromised and the impact of the tragedy on the delivery of services.

Put People First. People are a company's best asset, and companies must make every effort to ensure the physical safety and emotional well-being of all employees. CEOs should continue their emphasis on people by being flexible. Employees will need time off for grieving and resolving their own personal emotions. Small gatherings should be encouraged so people have an opportunity to bond, heal emotionally, and make sense of the unfamiliar. Part of putting people first is also informing others of how they can help those affected by the crisis.

Stand in for the Company. CEOs are the living surrogates for companies in times of crisis. They put a human face on institutions, large and small. Employees expect CEOs to act on their company's behalf, and CEOs' actions can have a lasting impression on the company's reputation. Employees also expect CEOs to show honest emotion and reveal their organization's character during times of crisis. This can be accomplished by publishing CEO-signed advertisements that express sympathy and support, providing complimentary services during a crisis to those affected by events, and providing volunteer services and making financial contributions to crisis-related charitable organizations. These gestures serve as symbolic reminders that financial leaders accept their expanded roles, which extend beyond their industry and include serving as stewards of the nation's prosperity and well-being.

Tend to Business. CEOs need to keep one eye on unfolding events and employee welfare and the other on business. "Man is made of ordinary things," the poet Friedrich Schiller wrote, "and habit is his nurse." Getting people back to their daily routines is necessary for a speedy recovery and for establishing a sense of control over uncertainty. CEOs need to infuse their organizations with calm and then challenge employees to get back to their desks, back on the phones, and back to their plans. Publicly referring to the company's vision and values often provides a welcome beacon of light during uncertain times. Setting the right tone as people slowly return to normal is the CEO's role, and never will it be so sorely tested as during times of a crisis.

Be Prepared and Expect the Unexpected. All CEOs should have crisis preparedness at the top of their agendas, especially while the crisis is still fresh in many minds. Now is the time for CEOs to review what was done right, what was done wrong, and what could have been done better. It is also time to plan for possible emergency situations – from the very small to the very large. CEOs should make evacuation and fire drills a priority. CEOs should set into practice a system for tracking employee travel, regularly reviewing office-security procedures and expanding emergency-communications plans. An emergency-response team should be assigned to prepare a crisis-preparedness plan – or dust off or fine-tune a plan that was rarely implemented. The plan may include emergency telephone numbers, toll-free help lines, and "dark sites" on both the intranet and the Internet that can be activated when necessary.

Establishing order and taking charge are critical during crises. CEOs are the guardians of their companies and must rally for all to see and hear. As Napoleon said, "A leader is a dealer in hope."

The manner in which New York City Mayor Rudolph Giuliani responded to the September 11 terrorist attacks serves as a striking example of how to approach crisis communications. Mayor Giuliani, who was the obvious and natural focal point for people's attention, was personally concerned for the people involved in the tragedy and kept them informed of events as they unfolded. He approached the crisis with compassion and humanitarianism, and served as the source of factual information without speculating on events. As a result, he struck a perfect balance between demonstrating compassion and communicating facts.

Innovative Public Relations

As the public relations industry evolves, it continues to give rise to new approaches and strategies for winning results for clients. Of the wide range of communications services public relations professionals provide, product campaigns are among the activities that apply some of the most innovative communications strategies.

A critical ingredient for success when animating product campaigns is the ability to identify a trend that will create a need for the product based upon relevance. Often, the product's developers research the product's niche before production. However, consumer packaged goods and products still need exciting, interesting, accessible, and innovative foundations to capture the public's attention. Public relations professionals need to create a personal connection between the public and the product – a program that takes advantage of the product's unique selling point and dovetails it with a trend. Accomplishing this requires not only an understanding of the product, its unique attributes, and its selling points, but it also requires an understanding of the public's specific position on the product.

Recognizing that corporate reputation is among a company's most valuable assets is also part of innovative public relations services. For example, if a company representative is speaking with the financial community, the public relations firm needs to make certain that when members of the financial community view the company and its future prospects, they have a complete understanding of the company's vision and future direction.

The chief executive's reputation and his or her ability to develop a top-notch senior-management team are also critical factors to consider when developing a company's communication initiatives. Security analyst presentations serve as a good example of how important these factors are. At the presentation, security analysts will listen to the chief executive's report on the company's performance, analyze the company's quarterly results and listen to the chief executive's answers to analysts' questions. The chief executive not only interprets company activity, but also delivers a sense of confidence and hope and the company's future goals. Communications help convey the chief executive's values and capabilities, while helping to interpret company activity and then create a foundation upon which future goals can be built. Analysts will make a judgment on whether the chief executive is trustworthy and able to deliver on his or her promises.

In addition, innovative public relations often include brainstorming sessions that serve as opportunities for groups of professionals to talk through and build upon shared, multiple ideas. Well-organized brainstorming sessions that feature the right mix of participants who generate the energy needed to uncover fresh approaches and innovative strategies can result in communications target audiences understand and strongly respond to.

Regarding changes in the industry, I would like a serious understanding between clients and agencies that client presentations – not capabilities presentations, but rather those with original ideas, recommendations, strategic thinking, or creative work – are paid for by prospective clients. I believe public relations firms would approach the assignment more thoughtfully and that clients would receive an even better work product. Public relations firms have one key asset – their people, combined with their individual and collective experiences. To give that away doesn't make sense.

Success in Public Relations

To succeed in public relations, a person must approach communicating with the public from the perspective that individuals have the inherent ability to make the right decision for themselves, as long as they possess a strong foundation upon which to base those decisions. The information that a public relations professional provides the public should reflect this perspective and be presented with honesty and respect for others' beliefs. Spinning information is disrespectful to others because it presumes a person can manipulate the decisions of others. Successful public relations relies on setting priorities and keeping the public perspective a top priority.

Having a high degree of respect for an individual's ability to develop information from his or her own perspective results in the public relations professional providing useful information. If individuals receive useful information in an interesting, creative, engaging, and exciting way, then they will be far more likely to listen to it, absorb it, process it, and make decisions based upon it, whether they are stock-purchase, career, or political decisions.

Communications with the public must also be straightforward. Public relations professionals need to have the ability to step back from the situation and determine whether their target audience members received and understood the message they delivered, were able to act upon the message, and obtained value as a result of their services. Delivering value can be anything from selling cases of shampoo to raising investor confidence in a company.

The following guidelines can assist public relations professionals when creating communications that are both timely and relevant to their target audience:

❑ Read newspapers, magazines, and books; watch television; listen to the radio; go online; and become media savvy.
❑ Supplement participation in local industry events with professional and social activities in other industries and regions to understand what is appreciated and desired in different markets.
❑ Understand different attitudes and behaviors, while also recognizing the unique position of target audiences.

This understanding helps public relations professionals develop a unique, innovative campaign that meets the client's objectives.

❏ Obtain insight into specific media. Public relations professionals work through the media and other third parties to win media coverage and deliver an understanding of what a particular company does and why.

People need three key skills if they want to lead a public relations firm. First, being responsible for a client relationship of some size, probably larger than $1 million in fee income. Second, gaining international experience. Third, managing a P&L – managing a business to make a profit so that there is a return for investors.

From a broader perspective, motivating, developing, and properly managing people are critical skills. You have to communicate clearly and often. And you absolutely must understand what's on their minds. After all, in public relations, people are our product.

The greatest challenge international firms face is building and shaping knowledge, as well as best practices, across the globe. This means public relations professionals have to be equally sophisticated everywhere in the world in how they work for clients, regardless of where or when. This also means they have to operate 24/7. Sometimes this can be difficult, but it is what the international or global client wants.

What this means for our firm is twofold: First, the scope of the work and the expectation must be clear and realistic. Second, we must commit ourselves to a different kind of training – we need to use technology to transfer more and more knowledge to our people around the world. We must also have a team at the ready, so they can act quickly and flexibly in sending talented staff to other parts of the world to help our staff learn, grow, and develop the skills the client expects of them. This makes knowledge a key strategy for the future – developing it, sharing it, and making it available to every part of our world, all for the benefit of delivering value to the client.

For this reason, knowledge is a key strategic platform for our firm. We have built our own online university, with client-devoted intranet sites to share skills around the world, pioneer our own original research into reputation and the Internet, and devote considerable resources to training.

Because of external circumstances and because public relations is not performed in a vacuum, there are no specific, traditional standards to measure success, such as frequency in reach, which is used to gauge success in advertising. Some public relations companies use shareholder, consumer awareness, customer and employee satisfaction, and public-opinion surveys to measure the success of their programs. Ideally, the first survey is performed before the campaign begins, with the second survey performed six to eight months later to track the campaign's progress. Because of the expense, however, companies are often reluctant to make the necessary investment. In addition, many companies prefer to survey the reputation of a brand – its relevance in the marketplace and distinguishing features. But results can be unreliable because of the tremendous influence advertising has on a brand.

Although it may be difficult for a public relations firm to measure the success of a campaign, a proven approach is not the number of times a particular audience received a particular message, but rather the quality of the message and the target audience member's actions that were based upon it. Success also lies in understanding the client and the public, and the public relations company's ability to blend with the client.

Public relations has become both art and science – the research makes it a science, and the understanding of the public makes it an art. The need to have a strong grasp of the corporate mission is underscored by behavior. The public relations professional must understand the messages a company wants to communicate and, just as importantly, who the desired public is, what their perceptions are, what they believe is the real story, and what type of information they need or want to make a particular decision. Real public relations understands the message from a corporate standpoint, but also from the individual's standpoint – specifically, where he or she is in terms of the company's perceptions. To achieve success in public relations, these perceptions must be addressed directly and honestly.

Christopher P. A. Komisarjevsky is president and chief executive officer of Burson-Marsteller Worldwide, one of the world's leading communications consulting firms. Before joining Burson-Marsteller in 1995, Mr. Komisarjevsky was president and chief executive officer of Gavin Anderson & Company, a public relations subsidiary of Omnicom, and was responsible for the firm's U.S. operations.

Before Gavin Anderson, Mr. Komisarjevsky held a series of senior leadership positions at Hill and Knowlton, Inc. During his 20-year career there, he served as president and chief executive officer of the firm's Europe, Middle East, and Africa operations, and chief executive of its Carl Byoir & Associates subsidiary. Mr. Komisarjevsky also served as head of the firm's New York office and Corporate Practice.

Mr. Komisarjevsky has been responsible for public relations and public affairs activities for major corporate and trade association clients in a number of industries, including financial services, building materials, entertainment, pharmaceuticals, healthcare, communications, real estate, management consulting, and consumer products. He also has extensive experience in crisis management and labor negotiations.

In addition to being a widely published author of articles on a variety of public relations topics, Mr. Komisarjevsky has lectured on communications and business at Spain's Instituto de Empresa, Switzerland's International Institute for Management Development, and the New York University Graduate School.

Mr. Komisarjevsky holds a master's degree in business administration, has performed graduate work in German literature and international affairs in the United States and Europe, has attended the Wharton School, and holds a bachelor's degree in political science.

A 1996 recipient of the Ellis Island Medal of Honor, Mr. Komisarjevsky serves on the boards of a number of not-for-profit organizations and is a trustee of EQ Advisors Trust.

Mr. Komisarjevsky also served in the U.S. Army from 1967 to 1972 as a captain, helicopter pilot, instructor pilot, flight commander, and plans officer, serving in Vietnam with the First Cavalry Division in 1969 and 1970.

THE CREATION OF TRUST

RICH JERNSTEDT
Golin/Harris International
Chief Executive Officer

Trust Building vs. Publicity

Public relations is being redefined to include a much more strategic definition and, importantly, a much more strategic role than most people associate with it.

It isn't just publicity anymore – not that publicity isn't important. One of the major reasons public relations counselors are involved in an issue (or an opportunity) is to either generate exposure through publicity or to prevent exposure in the media. It will always be an important function of public relations. However, today, public relations as a discipline and public relations people as professionals can provide many new services, talents, and overall contributions.

It explains why some people and companies are moving away from the words "public relations" to identify communications departments or communications programs. They are using other words to describe this function that are broader and more strategic. Terms such as "communications," "corporate relations," and "reputation management" are being used to identify the public relations function. The traditional perception of public relations is too limited, too tactical, and too, well, traditional.

Actually, I am happy with the title "public relations," as long as it is perceived as being as big and broad and important as it really is. In the past, public relations was very tactical in its orientation – the "PR guy or gal" wrote releases, developed speeches, created collateral material, staged events, generated media coverage, and handled other tactics of communications for clients. More recently, public relations has been involved in more of the strategic solutions for clients. The "PR person" has helped decide the role the communications function should play by interacting with other disciplines inside a company, such as human resources, marketing, public affairs, law, finance, and government relations. With this in mind, it seems logical in today's world that the "public relations professional" is moving naturally into the policy-making area. Whether it's as the communications experts or not, communications people are playing a critical role at the table along with other senior executives representing all the other important disciplines required to lead the company successfully.

Communications people have earned this role over the years. They are invited to participate – not because a news release has to be written, or even to determine the specific role for communications – but because they bring critical thinking skills, knowledge of the industry, experience in similar situations, and insight into the company – and, I believe, because communications people typically think more broadly and with a holistic attitude. It makes the public relations professional more analytical, discipline-neutral, and sensitive to input – whether it's research, instincts, or simply listening to others for clues that will solve problems.

The communications person can also be counted on to encourage communications internally, so there is positive interaction that results in the best solutions. By understanding the concept of a "best teams" approach, the public relations person helps ensure that no one discipline or no one individual has any more influence than is appropriate.

All these talents are typically inherent in a communications person. It has resulted in senior management wanting the communications person to be a part of the team that creates and manages solutions to challenges and opportunities that exist in every company.

Another important dynamic that has elevated the role of the public relations counselor is the growing recognition of the importance of communications. Smart communications strategies must be at the foundation of every smart business decision. And, many times, it is a challenge. There are competing messages, lack of understanding, too much information, too many information channels, not enough time to comprehend, no willingness to find the time. But more and more, everyone wants to make an informed decision.

Public relations people who understand how to solve problems, how to develop relevant messages, and how to deliver those messages in a high-impact way to the right audiences deserve to be on the senior management team.

Getting at the Emotions

The goal of a successful public relations professional has changed over the years. It used to be providing exposure. Then it moved from not just providing exposure, but encouraging an understanding. The next evolutionary step is not only to provide understanding, but also to create a sense of advocacy. At our firm, we believe the best way to accomplish this goal is through the creation of trust.

So the challenge is to move the constituents – whether they are employees, shareholders, neighbors of the plant, government regulators, or the consumers – not only to be aware of the product, and not just to understand what the product does, but to want to make that product, service, or company a part of their purchase habits and a part of their lifestyle – and, importantly, to advocate that others should feel and do the same. This is one of the things that public relations can do so much better than other communications disciplines. It is inherent in public relations to get at the emotion, the credibility, the need to understand, and the desire to take action.

The fundamental role of a public relations person is to deliver results. Demonstrating that our communications strategies – when executed effectively to the key audiences – create the desired action must be our primary goal.

Communications Synergy for Best Effect

On the agency side, success for a public relations professional can be measured by everything from a thank you from the client, to a client renewing a contract, or the client giving you more to do because he realizes you get results. At another level, it includes having research that indicates you did move the needle on awareness or attitudes. At still another level, it is the methodology to track increases in sales or the increase in share price or positive scores in a survey of employees that are all the direct result of public relations activities.

With this in mind, there are some very quantifiable measurements that can be employed, with time and other resources. It is a myth that you can't track the results of public relations, although, because of the influences of other forms of communications activities, such as direct marketing, event marketing, and advertising, it may be very difficult to determine what impact the public relations programming itself had.

In fact, public relations can be at its most valuable by working synergistically with other communications activities. It can be argued that public relations helps the other forms of communications be that much more effective. For instance, the consumer might be more willing to pay attention to the 30-second commercial if he or she read a story about the product earlier in the day. You might open the envelope you received in the mail – not thinking of it as junk mail – if you realize it's more information about the product you just read about in a newspaper or magazine, or saw demonstrated on a television talk show.

An interesting development in public relations is the use of "non traditional" tactics. They are "non traditional" because public relations people typically were not expected to provide the counsel or the execution of these tactics, and because they are totally new techniques – sometimes driven by new technology – to reach people effectively.

Because people are overwhelmed by the choices of television channels and don't have the time to read the newspaper or magazine or even access the Internet to keep up-to-date on the news, public relations people have begun to use other ways of reaching the client's target audience more than ever before. So now, event marketing and buzz marketing are techniques that a PR professional employs to ensure the right messages are getting to the right people in more ways than just through media coverage. And the use of sales promotion, direct marketing, and even advertising can be found in the overall planning of a public relations campaign.

The Internet should also be the responsibility of the public relations experts. It's all about being interactive. That's what public relations people do.

No matter what it takes, the public relations professional must develop programming that delivers measurable results. This requires agreement on what results are to be achieved and on applying resources to develop appropriate measurement techniques.

Commit to Measure

The first step to measuring a return on an investment in public relations is to find out what your client will recognize as a valid, worthwhile, or credible return. Every client is a bit different. Some clients measure success by the amount of publicity coverage. Others measure success by the quality of that coverage. Others measure it by determining what happened as a result of that quality coverage. Still others go right to sales figures and want to know what can justifiably be attributed to the role of public relations.

Public relations people are becoming as smart and resourceful as their advertising partners in the development of measurement techniques or devices the client or senior management will recognize as valid. Part of that is a function of the growing size of public relations budgets. It is easier to allocate dollars for research when the total amount of money to be spent reaches significant amounts.

I'm reminded of an association client who asked us early in the relationship to meet for a day of planning. One group met with the market research experts of the companies that made up the association in one room, and another met with the communications experts of these member companies in an adjoining room. The objective at the end of the day was to determine how to spend the million-dollar program budget and measure its impact. The communicators created a million-dollar program in one room, and the market research people created a $300,000 measurement program to evaluate the success of the program in the other room. When we got together, we realized measuring the million-dollar program was going to require $300,000, so now we only had a $700,000 program – and lots of discussion on whether to spend the $300,000 to measure it.

The answer, by the way, was "no." But we did create a series of very effective measurement tools for that program because there was a commitment to do it right. Over time, a number of very sophisticated evaluation methods have been developed for public relations. Both output and outcomes can be tracked with high degrees of detail. The application of technology – especially the Internet – has been particularly important.

Since trust between our firm and our clients is also an important goal, we know that a strong commitment to measurement is key. The return on the communication investment is as important as all other forms of investment.

Building – and Busting – Trust

One advantage public relations has over all other forms of communications activities is the way it informs people about the client's message. I believe people are more willing to learn more comprehensively through the tactics of public relations. For example, if I am at home reading my mail, I am not willing to stop to read a long promotion piece. I am going through my mail. If I am watching my television, I can't learn enough in a 30-second spot. One thing I think public relations does very well is provide in-depth and comprehensive information.

The second is that it provides an endorsement of the product or service that is not inherent in advertising. If I read an article in a newspaper or listen to a spokesperson on a television talk show or hear about a product from a family member whose opinion I respect, that endorsement and the credibility associated with it give that message a very strong impact.

In addition to that, there's also an emotional bond that can be generated through the techniques of public relations. It's not that a 30-second spot can't tug at your heartstrings, but the tactics of public relations have a way of ensuring that emotional bonds are created between a customer and the product, or the employee and the employer.

It basically comes down to the concept of trust, which is the most all-inclusive dynamic that should exist between a communicator and the receiver of that communication. If it is prevalent, it generates loyalty, a sense of credibility, and a sense of dependability. More importantly, it gives a sense of confidence and advocacy that will withstand challenges or temptations that could affect the bond.

In other words, it's generating goodwill between a brand and the consumer. Because of the trust instilled in the relationship, the individual will doubt whether bad news about the brand can be true before making any conclusions, and will grant the company or the brand a chance to correct itself if necessary – and will accept an apology.

We call this the TrustBank. Our founder, Al Golin, and the founder of McDonald's Corporation, Ray Kroc, created this concept years ago. Simply stated, it is doing the right thing to build goodwill with your key audiences. It includes everything from sponsoring sports teams and school programs in local communities to making responsible decisions in times of a global crisis.

The equity that builds up over time is invaluable in preserving the trust that must exist between a company or brand (or even an individual) and the audiences that are critical to the success of the brand.

We have created a variety of other tools that help us work with clients to understand what they must do to create trust with their key constituents. Why is trust so important?

We see trust as being a "higher" concept than reputation or image. Trust drives reputation. And image is just one aspect of the dynamic of trust. The critical elements of trust are integrity, competence, affinity, reinforcement, leadership, and commitment. It is an emotional bond that is personal, one-to-one, and lasting.

Here is a list of behaviors we identified with Jim Lukaszewski, a highly regarded communications consultant, that do NOT build trust. We call them "Trust Busters."

Arrogance	Holding back
Broken promises	Ignoring killer questions
Chest beating	Ignoring core values
Creating fear	Lies
Deception	Minimizing danger
Denial	Negative surprises
Disparaging the opposition	Stalling
Disrespect	Underrating negative emotion

Failure to seek forgiveness   Overrating preparation
Ducking responsibility   Victim confusion

Don't be victimized by these Trust Busters.

The Five Cs of Successful Branding

Public relations adds context, texture, emotion, and definition to a brand, so the audience – whether it's a customer, an employee, or a shareholder – can develop the trust that needs to exist with the brand. It is based on having enough information to make a choice, an individual choice, about how one feels about this brand. It's all about accessing information from a credible source, so an individual can make a decision about how to feel about a brand.

The greatest brands in the world achieved the status by following what our firm calls the Five C's of Successful Branding.

First of all, one has to have a compelling proposition that's high-impact and relevant. It has to mean something of importance.

The second element in building a successful brand is to be sure there is some way of distinguishing between it and other brands that may compete for the same or similar positioning. In other words, there is a clear and distinctive position that is yours alone. If you stand for something, you stand out. By understanding what is truly unique about your organization, or brand, and staying focused on it, you define and then own the position. You can't be all things to all people, so narrow the focus appropriately. If you narrow your focus, you expand your impact.

The third C is that there must be consistent delivery of the brand promise. It can be trusted and relied upon every day and in every place. Communicate what you are about…and communicate it again. It requires some discipline, of course, and maybe some creativity to find different ways to communicate the same promise.

The fourth is a connection with the stakeholders. More simply put, there has to be a meaningful and emotional bond. Care about what they care about.

And fifth is a commitment to leadership and innovation. Your brand will be important in an ever-changing environment and can be trusted today and tomorrow. It means meeting or exceeding the expectations of your key audiences. And it means setting the bar for your competition. Ironically, it may mean joining with your competition to solve large issues. It certainly means changing as necessary, to continually strive for excellence in everything the brand means.

What's the Big Idea?

For a public relations campaign to be energized and come to life, there has to be a Big Idea.

Although the Big Idea doesn't have to be expensive, it has to have the ability to deliver its message through the clutter, the confusion, and the overwhelming amount of information people are exposed to. So the Big Idea may be very simple, but it is compelling.

More important, a variety of communication strategies can be developed around the Big Idea that leads to a program that really works on a variety of levels to achieve all the goals set.

The second answer to how to create a Big Idea is to develop an Acceptable Idea that generates support from all those involved to make it work. I've seen many average concepts work in a big way because everyone was aligned to ensure success. In the end, it was a Big Idea because it achieved the goal.

Agency people, especially, have to know a Big Idea is only as good as its ability to be sold in. You certainly cannot be afraid to sell and sell hard if you are convinced your thinking is right. But if your client does not agree, add some resourcefulness to your creativity. Determine what it will take to get the buy-in you need. Ensure that buy-in comes with commitments of time, energy, budget, staffing, and support.

To come up with the Big Idea in a public relations campaign, you have to have access to information and the analytical talents required to review the information effectively. It is having a history or experience with a product, the audience, the category, or the geography that helps us get to that Big Idea. And it is having some insight, instincts, and intuition. Some magic doesn't hurt. And a little luck can be useful!

A successful public relations professional has to set the parameters that help define where and how the Big Idea has to work. In other words, he or she has to know what the limits or boundaries are. Is it geographical? Is it by audience? By budget? Is it by brand characteristics? Or is it by action that results from exposure to the messages behind the Big Idea? Usually, it's a combination of all these to some degree.

After the boundaries are known and agreed upon, the creativity takes over. Inside those parameters, you want people to be wildly creative. If the parameters are correct, it is comforting to know that any idea generated will be on target. Find the idea that is not only on target, but that also will motivate the team whose job it is to make it work. And, of course, be sure the idea will motivate the audience to act in a way that will meet your communications and business objectives.

Public Relations Goes Global

Public relations doesn't necessarily have to be different on a global level. The objective for effective global planning is to understand the overall message and how it needs to be communicated everywhere to be supporting and reinforcing. It is the understanding of the message that must be consistent. If the message itself is delivered in the same way everywhere, language differences alone will make it inconsistent – not to mention the cultural differences.

Having an understanding of the local markets in which the message must resonate helps you understand the best way to execute the overall program. It isn't like it used to be, when global was thought to be the same way every place. Global now means the program must be executed at the local level, with rewording or redefining as appropriate to the local market. Of course, it is all based on the global direction.

Accordingly, people are now referring to global as multi-national, or "glocal," to indicate recognition that a combination of both local and global input in the development and execution of a program, market by market, around the world, is required. I have a grid to help clients track where they are or want to be in creating and executing their global initiatives.

The vertical bar moves from being centralized to decentralized, left to right, in the development of strategies. Then the horizontal bar moves from being local on the bottom to global at the top to determine how the tactics of the program are being executed, so you are able to plot where the influences are coming from. In some programs, it may be a very centralized strategy and executed the same way all over the world. In other circumstances, you might find the strategy is developed at a local level and executed at the local level. To do this plotting, you have to find out where the decision-maker is, where the budget is controlled, and where the influences are that need to be factored in for the program to be successful every place in the world. If you don't know, the grid can help you find out.

Listen . . . Learn

The best piece of advice I have ever received can be stated in one word: Listen. Listen to the client, for understanding the need or the opportunity that he or she is addressing. And listen to all the sources of information that need to be factored in to form the basis of a recommendation.

Part of listening includes being aware and involved in what's going on around you. You can't be a very successful practitioner if you're not aware of what's happening in the world. This involves listening, watching, and even participating to make sure you are well versed on what you need to know to provide the best counsel.

Maybe this advice is so relevant to public relations people because we tend to express ourselves well, either in writing or orally, or both. To be an effective communicator, we all learned early on, you have to understand it is two-way. While you give someone else the chance to communicate, you have to listen!

Who said that God gave public relations people two ears and two eyes, but only one mouth for a very good reason?

The advice I find myself most often giving is to be aware and informed about everything that may be involved in your communications assignment. Bring as much as you can into the situation by maintaining a high level of awareness of what is going on in your world. Then, be able to determine what you have to learn, and find out how you can learn all you need to know – usually fast. Finally, know how to use the information to make informed, strategic recommendations.

You do not have to be an expert on everything. Know what you know, and know what you don't know.

Seven Truths

For me, the "golden rules of public relations" is a list I keep updated called the "Seven Truths." They change as the world changes.

The first truth is Insight. As mentioned, you have to understand everything about the situation to develop the best public relations counsel. What are the political, economic, social influences? How does your audience receive its news? What interests and motivates your audiences? How is your audience the same and different in all parts of the world? What information do you need to uncover The Big Idea? Insight not only gives you an in-depth look at all parts of the situation, but it also helps you adjust and anticipate problems and opportunities.

We are getting better all the time at determining what kind of input we need and how to analyze it. For example, the engagement of cultural anthropologists is an interesting development that helps uncover and process behaviors that enhance our insight.

The next truth is Speed. It is an understanding that everything – information, travel, trade, innovation, and competition – is working faster than ever before. The old public relations saying of "I'll get back to you" just doesn't work anymore. Decisions must be made quickly, and communications dealt with carefully, accurately, and, often, immediately. Technology makes everything fast; use it to your advantage. Internet, intranet, satellites, webcasts, and e-mails all help provide fast management of information.

The third truth is Alliances. More than ever before, companies are coming together to cooperate and achieve an objective they might not have been able to achieve on their own either as fast or as efficiently. *Forbes* recently referred to this as one of the most powerful trends that has swept American business in a century. You see expressions like "partner or perish" and "collaborate or die" or "co-opetition," cooperating with the competition. Recognize that through collaboration, a company's goals can be reached, because of a common geography, a common target audience, common brand characteristics, or complementary strengths and weaknesses. Through partnering with another company, a product or service has access to the other's existing credibility.

Another reason alliances make sense in today's world is that collaboration drives innovation. Combining teams who typically act and think differently will result in new ideas.

The fourth truth I refer to as Relevance. It's understanding that the unique selling proposition or the sustainable competitive advantage is what ensures that your brand will be distinct enough to be understood, remembered, and supported. For example, Gerber is the baby food company that positions the health and welfare of babies first;

McDonald's is known as the world's best quick-service restaurant experience that makes you smile every time.

The fifth element relates to the Architecture that helps you monitor, manage, and lead for success. It's understanding who defines strategy, who controls the budget, what resources exist, where they are, and who controls them, as well as the processes that are in place. It's critical to remember that this must be changed often. If it isn't changed, you are falling behind, or you run the risk of maintaining an environment that is not stimulating to your most important asset, your people.

The organization that works must include a foundation for knowledge management. Develop the systems that ensure information is collected, transferred, updated, and accessible.

The sixth truth is Integrated Communications, or the understanding that the best way to communicate is integrating all forms of communications. It is determining who will take the lead or who will help decide the role that each of these communications disciplines will play. You have to remember the target audience doesn't know or remember or care how they were informed. So the integration or the interconnected nature of the disciplines is an important criterion to ensure you are using resources effectively.

As mentioned earlier, since public relations people tend to take a comprehensive view of the world, there is a real opportunity for public relations people to be in the center of all these other communications disciplines. Public relations professionals tend to think in a more media-neutral way, which helps qualify them to lead all the others. We think strategically and holistically and can be trusted to develop fact-based plans. As public relations professionals, we know the interactive arena better, because we are famous for interactive communications.

The seventh truth is the role of Multidimensional Communications. This is a corollary to the "integrated" truth. Communications today must work on a variety of levels. The "experiential" dynamic is critical, for example – reaching the target audience in an environment that is most compelling to receive and act upon the message. Is it the point of sweat? Is it the point of stroke? The point of hunger? The point of romance? The point of fun? The point of family?

Getting to that critical place ensures that you are using a variety of emotions and senses to communicate most effectively – feeling, thinking, sensing, smelling, hearing, and most importantly, being involved, or acting. For many of our clients, public relations professionals show what it takes to create programs that provide an opportunity for the target audience to actually experience the product, the message, or the excitement, so they not only listen, but they also remember it and act on it.

Making a Difference in the Future

In the future, public relations will more fully evolve into a management discipline that will be treated very seriously and importantly by everybody.

The role of communications and the exchange of information will be seen as the most critical indicators of a company's success. People who understand how to influence the process will be critical to senior management and, more often, will become the most senior management.

The roles that communications people will play will be much broader than they are today. It will be assumed that the public relations professional will deliver the policy-making counsel that leads to the strategic planning. The public relations person will also have access to a wider variety of communications tools and tactics than ever before to execute against the strategies. Because the practitioners will participate in critical decisions at very senior levels, the entire profession will be elevated and motivated by the opportunity to make a real difference in everything we do.

And public relations will still be fun because it's "fun" to be important and to be involved in important issues. And it's fun to be the expert in understanding how to develop trust with people that leads to achieving your goals.

Rich Jernstedt is chief executive officer of Golin/Harris International. He has played a lead role in the growing success of the company since his appointment in 1991. From its origins as a single Chicago office to its current place among the world's top marketing communications firms, under Mr. Jernstedt's leadership G/H has become a growing, dynamic enterprise that builds strong, trust-based relationships with its clients and employees.

On the client side, Mr. Jernstedt has proved himself one of the preeminent strategic and tactical thinkers in the world of consumer branding and product marketing. Throughout his 24-year career at G/H, Mr. Jernstedt has overseen client programs in such specialty areas as crisis management, consumer marketing, health and medical, corporate communications, branding, and reputation management. His counseling to clients has represented some of the world's leading brands, including McDonald's Corporation, Levi Strauss & Co., Sony Corporation, Campbell's Soup, Citicorp, and DaimlerChrysler.

Mr. Jernstedt plays an integral role in G/H's aggressive acquisitions initiative, further extending the company's reach and its ability to serve clients around the globe through new resources in Europe, the Middle East, Africa, Latin America, and Asia.

Before joining Golin/Harris, Mr. Jernstedt spent five years in corporate marketing communications with Container Corporation of America. He also served for three years as a Navy public affairs officer on aircraft carriers in the Western Pacific and the Mediterranean.

Mr. Jernstedt is a member of the boards of directors of the Council of Public Relations Firms and Off The Street Club and the board of trustees of the University of Oregon Foundation. He is listed in Who's Who in America. He is a frequent speaker on agency management and communications counseling at professional meetings and college campuses around the country.

A native Oregonian, Mr. Jernstedt is a 1969 journalism graduate of the University of Oregon.

THE NEW BREED OF THE INFORMED, PROACTIVE CONSUMER: THE PROSUMER

DON MIDDLEBERG
Middleberg Euro RSCG
Chairman and Chief Executive Officer

Defining Public Relations

Public relations is an art. And as an art, it has many definitions and components. Public relations can entail investor relations and employee communications. It can require influencing the influencers and managing consumer perceptions. It can include using communications to help companies manage crises and using communications to help companies manage change.

Helping companies manage change is especially important in today's ever-evolving business and economic landscape. As a result, the current definition of public relations must also include helping clients establish the right pace of communications; employ intelligence and research strategically; establish the right dialogue with the right audience; and finally, collaborate with a new breed of informed, proactive consumer – the *prosumer.*

New PR Imperatives

Innovation and technology have drastically altered the business landscape, and they have similarly changed the practice of PR. In today's fast-moving business environment, technology and innovation are driving business growth, and PR practices must not only reflect this new reality, but they must also leverage the tools and speed fueling this evolution. Leading PR executives know businesses need their communications partners to help them grow amid the changes being wrought by technology and innovation.

For PR, gone are the days of long-cycle planning, one-way communications, nominal expectations, and an audience of one (the journalist). Today's business landscape requires a new set of PR fundamentals that include:

Instantaneous planning: New technologies have increased the speed, reach, and efficiency of business. As a result, companies have found the forecasting and long-range cycles of the past ineffective. PR plans and strategies must reflect this change, and PR professionals must be prepared to develop new tactics and messaging as quickly as the market changes.

Audience-driven communications, business-driven communications and journalist-driven communications: As businesses court a wider variety of stakeholders, PR professionals must develop communications specifically targeted to all of a company's constituents. Communications aimed solely at the journalist will not achieve a company's business objectives.

Information flood: Consumers, journalists, investors, and businesses are all being flooded in the streams of the information technology revolution. As a result, many find it difficult, if not impossible, to stay abreast of new trends, technologies, and market shifts. PR people must continuously absorb and filter information on behalf of their clients and their clients' constituents to ensure that their clients' messaging stays relevant and credible amid the flood of new information.

Measurable ROI: As PR's contributions to brand awareness and competitive positioning gain more recognition, businesses are beginning to seek ways of measuring the results of their PR investments. PR professionals must develop campaigns that demonstrate hard results to key business decision-makers.

Successful PR campaigns today recruit outside influencers from a variety of disciplines, stay very brand-focused, and rely on integrated media relations teams that can speak the languages of business, technology, and the new prosumer equally well. To do this, agencies must follow a number of new truisms.

First, PR strategists must create flexible corporate positions and messages that can be quickly adapted to fast-emerging trends and market evolution. Because the business environment is changing at unprecedented speeds due to technological advances and innovation, corporate positions and messages must evolve to stay in step with the larger market developments. PR strategists must be vigilant in ensuring that their clients' messages and positioning stay resonant.

Second, they must rely on research and intelligence to understand how brands are perceived in the eyes of the media and other influencers. To develop the communications approach that will help clients reach their business objectives, it is critical for PR professionals to identify the perceptions a client's own executives hold of the company, as well as those held by the marketplace, analysts, and media; define the trends and issues relevant to the client's business; and uncover the positioning and messaging approaches that will set the client apart from competitors.

Third, they must never fall prey to "Buzz Word Bingo." In an environment characterized by jargon and information overload, PR professionals must create messages that are clear, concise, and intuitive. Simplicity wins in today's complex business environment.

Fourth, they must balance strategic planning with on-the-ground media relations and strategy execution from the start of every campaign. Intelligence gathering and strategic planning take time. But business and markets are changing fast. As a result, PR professionals must work to garner results at the start of a client engagement, while also focusing on longer-range strategies that will ensure sustained results.

Fifth, PR executives must use every message delivery channel available by fusing traditional and digital tactics into each campaign. As media outlets and communications tools proliferate, it becomes increasingly important for PR campaigns to reach constituents at every touch-point. PR professionals must become adept at using traditional channels, such as print and broadcast outlets, as well as new e-mail, webcast, and other technologically-enabled channels.

Sixth, they must develop campaigns that directly target a wider set of influencers and tastemakers to validate the client's brand leadership and maintain the perception of innovation. Journalists aren't the only audience businesses need to reach. Analysts, investors, employees, and consumers have prominent roles in the success of a company, and PR strategies must reach every audience that can contribute to a company's growth and position in the marketplace.

And last, but certainly not least, PR executives must encourage their clients to be open and honest in all communications.

Core Goal: Creating Positive Brand Awareness

Without question, public relations can build brands better than any other tool. According to Al Reiss, author of *The 22 Immutable Laws of Branding*, "The birth of a brand is usually accomplished with publicity, not advertising." PR used to be about creating publicity, but today it is about building and maintaining a company's brand in the eyes of a wide variety of stakeholders. To accomplish this, public relations executives must rely on research, industry intelligence, and analysis to fully understand how their clients' brands are perceived in the eyes of the media and influencer communities and then use this information to validate and grow brand leadership.

In addition, because of the speed of business and economic change, today's public relations professionals must know how to create flexible messaging that can be quickly adapted to fast-emerging trends and market evolution to ensure that their client's positioning resonates amid market changes. Campaigns must target the full range of client stakeholders – from analysts and media representatives, to investors and consumers – and must use every delivery channel available, including broadcast, print, and online outlets.

Although the specific goals of any campaign can differ dramatically, there is usually a common set of themes relevant to all clients to gain awareness. This is marketing 101, but building positive brand awareness is the core goal of every PR campaign. The second – and perhaps more important – point is that even though many clients are already well known, they need to get recognized for who they are *now*. We live in an age of accelerating change. The world is changing faster and faster, at a pace that is almost incomprehensible. Companies need to keep pace with the changes in the world. And they are. But the communication of that change often lags. Public relations professionals today are charged with helping companies communicate how they've changed. And that has become the most important goal of public relations – to develop innovative programs that help companies use communications to grow their businesses during periods of great change.

Reaching the Prosumer

Public relations and marketing today are more about the creative conversation than the direct sell. PR communicators must view their roles as creating an opportunity for ongoing interaction between their clients and their clients' many constituents. According to George Gallate, the CEO of Euro RSCG Interaction, "Branding must become a dialogue; a dialogue that shifts venues; a dialogue that is present and consistent at every point of contact – new and old."

Today's communicators must use technology and innovative strategies to make PR more effective. The dot-coms taught us that PR must fuse digital and traditional approaches to succeed in a changing marketplace. While the dot-com fires have cooled, the lessons learned still apply. To succeed in today's fast-moving, multi-channel business environment, PR professionals must fuse the best practices used to build Fortune 500 companies with those used to grow emerging companies. They must build traditional media relations programs and then bolster them with the innovative technological tactics enabled by the Internet, e-mail and the Web.

Communicators working for consumer companies must adopt a new role in facilitating a dialogue with today's new breed of proactive, empowered consumer – the prosumer. With more product choices, more media options, and greater access to information, today's consumers are able to exert far greater control over the purchasing process, as well as over the value of a company's brand. To meet the needs and demands of these prosumers, communicators must help their clients serve as true brand partners. To succeed at this, today's communicator must view the prosumer as a partner, rather than just the object of a communications effort. Today's communicators must think about which message points will sway the prosumer's opinion, rather than just build a transitory desire. And, most important, today's communicators must recognize that the prosumer has become our communications vehicle, since word of mouth is the most powerful form of marketing and PR available today.

To do this, PR and marketing campaigns must abandon the traditional consumerist approach of mass marketing, standard messaging, and one-way communication. Instead, today's communicators must facilitate a prosumerist approach that relies on narrowcasting, participative media and innovative, high-tech tactics, such as permission marketing, buzz marketing, and whisper campaigns.

Today's consumers fully understand their value and power as prosumers and demand their due in terms of access to information, top-notch customer service, and personalized messages. It is now the role of communicators not to simply broadcast messages, but to help facilitate dialogues between clients and prosumers.

Growing Respect for PR

In the last decade, public relations has gained prominence and respect. Before the 1990s, the marketplace was unfamiliar with PR; the industry was viewed as a place for professional outcasts; and PR was generally confined to publicity alone. In addition, communications were incredibly slow; market research and strategic planning practically nonexistent; and the fees for services very low. As a result, PR garnered little respect. In the early 1990s, however, the speed of communications got a boost from the fax machine, FedEx, and then e-mail and the Internet. PR began to gain more power and, subsequently, greater awareness. New specialties, such as public affairs, investor relations, and employee communications emerged, and the excellent results engendered by these initiatives helped to garner new respect for PR in general. Then, the information technology revolution took hold, changing business – and PR – forever and for the better. Technology made markets more efficient, sped innovation, and began driving business.

To keep pace with the changes, businesses and journalists began relying on PR professionals as never before. Increasingly, businesses are asking PR professionals to help them manage their businesses amid constant market evolution, as well as communicate those changes to their audiences and stakeholders. In addition, as companies become more and more dependent on brand-building to maintain and grow their competitive positioning, PR becomes an increasingly strategic asset. Analysts have estimated that in today's knowledge-based economy, intangible assets such as brand and competitive advantage can account for as much as 75 percent of a company's worth. And because there is no better way to build brand than through PR, the profession has gained strategic prominence and newfound respect in the eyes of industry leaders. Today, PR professionals are regarded as strategic business partners, rather than mere publicity lackeys.

The status of PR professionals has changed in the journalists' eyes, as well. Today, journalists need PR people more than they did 30 years ago. Before, journalists tended to have individual beats, and they had young journalists under them. In other words, journalists had a lot of time to do their own research. Today, journalists need

PR professionals for industry intelligence and context, for story ideas, information, and background materials.

When I started out, it was well known that a journalist wouldn't take a call from a public relations person, no matter who it was. Now, there's a level of respect among most journalists for what we do. They rely on us for ideas and context for stories. Public relations has grown tremendously since I started out in the 1970s. Why? Because we are successful. Why? Because we are strategic. Why? Because we have a lot of outlets and a lot of ways to get our message across now.

Defining Success in Public Relations

Lately, there has been much interest in measuring the return on a PR investment or in trying to measure the results of PR. This is a natural response to the growing recognition of the important role PR plays in building intangible assets, such as brand awareness and competitive advantage. Naturally, with so much riding on the company's brand, business leaders are seeking ways of measuring returns on the PR and marketing investments designed to boost those assets. At the moment, some companies (particularly in Australia) are beginning to work out ways of putting intangible assets on the balance sheets. If they are successful, standards for measuring the returns on investments in these assets will follow, and then brand-building efforts will be formally linked to shareholder value.

While no measurement standard exists right now, there are a few ways to measure the success of public relations campaigns. One is the quantitative approach of measuring the impact of an action. For example, if an article appears in a major publication, you can literally measure the sales that directly result from that article.

I used to represent Dreyfus, and the former director of marketing at Dreyfus asked me one afternoon – knowing we had secured an article that would run in *The Wall Street Journal* the next day on one their new funds – to come down to the Dreyfus offices the next morning. I got there at 7 a.m. and saw person after person coming in with *The Wall Street Journal* in hand, pointing to the article and saying, "I want to buy this mutual fund." Most of them didn't even know the name of the fund; they just pointed to the paper.

This quantitative measure holds for other arenas, as well. For example, you can measure calls to a client's 800 number or the number of hits to the Web site. There are ways to count the diffusion of message points, or to gauge how your client is positioned against the competition. There are as many different qualitative measures as there are target audiences. For instance, if your target audience is industry lobbyists, then your qualitative measure would be how prominent your client's voice becomes in DC legislation. Or, if your target audience is your client's employees, then the qualitative metrics to measure the success of the PR effort would include the drop in employee turnover or more successful recruitment efforts or an increase in the number of resumes received by your client's company or a place in *Fortune* magazine's annual "Best Companies to Work For" list. There are many quantitative metrics for measuring the impact of public relations.

There are also qualitative ways of measuring the impact of a public relations campaign. This is what I call the "You'll Know" measurement because your client will know if their PR is working. How? The client will hear it from his or her mother, friends, neighbors – even strangers. If you're a CEO in any business, you have to have a very good sense of what works and what doesn't work. Most CEOs are very intuitive. They can tell immediately whether a program will work or not. All of these programs can be measured by the quantitative and the qualitative "You'll Know" approach.

Fishing With Chameleons

To be a leader in public relations, you have to have a sense of when things change to manage your own business, as well as help your clients manage and reposition theirs. Nothing is the same forever. The economy changes;

businesses change; technology changes; there's so much change that the best public relations executives have to be a bit chameleon-like. They have to be able to move an agency in the direction of new opportunities and help their clients do the same. The concept is to fish where the fish are and to use more than one hook. In the early- and mid-1990s, the fish were technology companies. The Internet created an ocean of opportunity that was extremely well stocked with fish. But after the millennium, that ocean dried up. Now, new oceans of opportunity are emerging as healthcare and consumer goods become strong again. In such an environment, the CEO of a public relations agency has to be very sensitive to changes. You have to anticipate changes and be able to lead your agency and your clients in a new direction at a very quick pace.

In terms of personal traits, three things are intrinsic to the successful public relations professional, or any professional for that matter. The third most important thing is brains. Although the difference between a 119 IQ and a 128 IQ is not terribly significant, the successful PR pro must have some brain power. The second attribute is intellectual curiosity, with a lack of fear. A successful PR professional has to be prepared to become an expert on any subject. In public relations, you might handle anything from oil to technology to apple pie. You have to be able to absorb different information and communicate that information quickly. To succeed at this, the PR pro must have a nose for news and be very inquisitive; it's an innate talent you're

99

either born with or you're not. The most effective PR professionals like working with journalists, and they understand the news business. They also possess a gift for translating complex information into straightforward, easily accessible language. Those who excel at PR understand their client's target audience and craft messages that elicit an action or response from that target audience.

The most important attribute for success in public relations is the desire to work hard. These days, too many people come into the profession thinking if they understand some of the technical details of what we do, they will automatically be a huge success. And of course, the dot-com era encouraged some of that thinking, because a lot of young people had some success very early. But the bottom line in any industry, particularly public relations, is that you have to work really hard for a long period of time to build contacts, to learn how to write, to understand different clients, and just to be good at your profession. So seniority, dedication, and perseverance really matter in this business.

The Client's Role in a Campaign

Clients who take an active role in a public relations campaign are the best clients. A PR professional loves to represent clients who are proactive and innovative, who create new products or services, who pursue acquisitions or mergers, who hire exciting new people, and who plan exciting events and programs.

I am a great believer that a company or an agency reflects the personality of its CEO. If a company has a CEO who's ready to put you to sleep, it's going to be a greater challenge to develop an exciting PR program. But if you're representing a CEO who's exciting, dynamic, and supportive and, in effect, "gets it," then you have a client who's going to help you, and the odds are that you will be very successful. Give me a CEO who "gets it," who's involved, who has personality, and who is interesting and maybe even exciting, and I guarantee I'll give you a great PR program.

Needed: People Who Know People

The best piece of business advice I have ever received came from my grandmother. She said, "If you want something, you have to ask for it. If you don't ask, you don't get." If you think about that advice in terms of whether you want a story or a piece of business, you have to say, "I want your business." And if you don't say that – with enthusiasm and sincerity – you won't get the business.

Aside from asking for the business, the advice I find myself giving PR people most frequently is to read a lot. Keep current with all media. Be a student of the media.

Understand the media. Never pitch a story without reading the publication first. Try to understand what the journalists' interests are, who the journalists' readers are, and how the journalists have covered their beats in the past.

I also tell my people all the time that if they're having lunch every day at their desks, they are not doing their jobs. A PR professional's job is to get out there and meet people, to meet journalists, to meet their peers, to meet people in different walks of life. Essentially, a PR person's job is to get out and touch and feel. This is an age of high-tech and high-touch. Good PR professionals must have their antennae up for the way people are motivated, for what their interests are, what their needs will be, and how they will respond to them professionally.

The bottom line is that PR pros have to like people. If you don't like people in this business, you'll be very unsuccessful. You really have to enjoy making new contacts and learning about new people. You have to be interested in their lives. If you're that kind of person, I think you can do well in this business. While you do need to have other qualifications, such as writing well, speaking properly, and acting professionally, you absolutely must have a great sensitivity to other people's needs.

Tuning into the needs of people is the ability to read people. It's an ability to adjust your personality to the people around you, so if someone is most comfortable with a low-key, quiet, reserved person, you can be that type of person. If someone likes people to be a bit more boisterous, a little more upfront, slightly more demanding, you can do that, as well.

When you have people working under you, you have to know when someone needs a pat on the back, or when someone needs a push. That's a skill you pick up over time. Some people are very good people-judgers, but the longer you're in public relations, the better you succeed at tuning in to people's needs and personalities.

A good PR leader possesses an ability to read people, as well as a skill for nurturing their trust in you. And in the end, that's what this game is about. You can have the greatest ideas in the world and the smartest propositions in the world, but if you don't have people who trust you and regard you as honest and credible, then you will never be able to get those ideas through.

The Bright Future of Public Relations

As public relations increases in effectiveness and strategic importance, PR professionals are being given an unprecedented opportunity to contribute to the growth and health of their clients' businesses. But with this great opportunity comes new responsibility.

For the future, PR professionals must strive to canonize and uphold the standards and tools that have allowed PR to gain prominence and respect. PR professionals must continue to work hard to ensure that all the information they disseminate on behalf of their clients is honest and credible. They must continuously anticipate economic, cultural, and social change and devise ways of helping their clients respond intelligently and proactively to those changes. They must remain open to the new tools that will help them function more efficiently and effectively for their clients. And they must constantly devise innovative strategies for communicating clients' messages and reaching their audiences.

PR executives of the future must fully embrace their new role as strategic partner to their clients, their clients' audiences, and journalists and work hard to provide those partners with intelligent, forward-looking information.

In a more tactical vein, PR professionals should start seeking opportunities to join a corporate, public, or advisory board. Lawyers, accountants, and other professionals routinely seek membership on corporate boards, and so should public relations professionals. In fact, I can't believe, in this age of crisis communications, there isn't a PR person on most boards, which goes hand-in-hand with building prominence for PR practitioners.

As we achieve positions on boards and increase our collective profile, public relations will begin to become a greater force – and we're beginning to see it now – on the academic level. More schools are beginning to introduce public relations courses. You're beginning to see schools such as Northwestern, USC, Florida, Georgia, Boston University, and Columbia getting involved in public relations. Now at least a dozen of the top schools have great communications programs, in which students can major in public relations, or at least learn very good communication skills by combining coursework in journalism with a communications degree.

In the future, we'll begin to see greater numbers of savvy professionals teaching PR programs correctly. Very often, public relations courses are taught by people who have or had careers in other professions, such as journalism. I would like to see public relations people retire and get into the top universities to teach what public relations in practice is all about. It has to start at the college level. The second change is a slow and steady upgrade of the profession. With that will come a continued upgrade in the perception of the profession.

When I started in PR, no one knew what public relations was, and no one really thought about it as a career. It was always the industry for the black sheep of the family; it was the place where you put people who couldn't cut it elsewhere. No wonder we've had to fight so hard for respect. But the tide has already started to turn to reflect the new status of public relations. According to a recent *Fortune* magazine piece, public relations is one of the top 15 desired careers. To be among the top 15 careers is astounding in terms of where we were coming from just 15 years ago. Young people want and understand public relations. As young people enter the professional ranks – whether they stay in PR or move into other services – the idea is that there will be a greater appreciation of public relations, because it's starting earlier in the schools. As a result, the future of PR is exceedingly bright.

Don Middleberg is widely regarded as one of the nation's leading public relations executives. As founder, chairman, and CEO of Middleberg Euro RSCG, Mr. Middleberg is responsible for some of the most successful and creative communications programs for clients such as American Express, Consumer Reports, Gartner Inc., IBM, Reuters, Sony Electronics, and United Airlines.

One of the most innovative PR executives and a "guru" on digital public relations, Mr. Middleberg was one of the first public relations practitioners to recognize and understand the impact the Internet would have on public relations. Mr. Middleberg is also the author of Winning PR in the Wired World.

Additionally, Mr. Middleberg co-authors, with Professor Steven Ross of the Columbia University Graduate School of Journalism, "The Middleberg/Ross Survey of Media in the Wired World," a groundbreaking and highly publicized survey of the nation's print and broadcast media and their use of the Internet.

A noted lecturer on public relations, Mr. Middleberg appears regularly before industry and educational forums. Consistently graded by program directors as among the best speakers in the country, he has addressed The Arthur Page Society, The Public Relations Society of America, The Financial Communications Society, and audiences at New York University, Boston University, and Cornell University. Mr. Middleberg is regularly called upon for commentary by magazines and newspapers and makes appearances on CNBC, C/Net, CNN, and National Public Radio.

Mr. Middleberg holds a bachelor's degree in economics and a master's degree in business administration in marketing.

PUBLIC RELATIONS AS AN ART AND A CRAFT

RON WATT, SR.
Watt/Fleishman-Hillard Inc./Cleveland
Chairman and
Chief Executive Officer

Strategies for Success in PR – The Reality

Public relations is an art and a craft. I am not sure it is a science. Many public relations people treat it as a scientific field and say they can measure this or that. You can probably do that to a degree, but even medicine – which is a science – cannot claim their methods will work from one patient to the next. So how can we be so scientific if even the scientific sciences admit that they are not?

You have to treat the field as an art and a craft. The ability to write well means you can think well, and we often do not see good writers anymore, just tacticians. Many agencies have developed useful ways of measuring things, and we use them, as well. It helps make the client feel they are getting their money's worth. But when you get to the true point of it, if the client's product is not selling, the service is not selling, or the position is not being communicated, why bother with any other measurement?

Ten or 15 years ago the Public Relations Society of America, with which I have been very much involved, came out with a study giving the definition of public relations. About 15 or 20 people wrote the page-and-a-half-long piece, and a couple of lawyers anointed it. The piece was vague and complicated, and it annoyed me to no end: How could we as an industry come up with such a complex and unclear definition? Our field gets itself into trouble because it thinks in terms that are not sharp and clear. We should be the bastions of clarity and simplicity. I once heard somebody say you should make your presentation "like Sesame Street." Make your presentation simple and get offstage as quickly as you can.

When setting up a campaign, the most important thing is for the campaign to be different from other campaigns. It should not be a rip-off of a campaign somebody else did. When you identify the company's product or position, you carefully assess the audiences and the constituencies, and you ask: "What do the audiences want? What are they interested in? Are they going to be interested in this product if we convey the information about the product properly?" The customer is still king. Public relations people often forget that. If you give the customer what the customer needs or wants through a campaign, the campaign will be successful. It is that simple.

One of the important goals of a campaign is for the client to feel they got their money's worth. But the main goal is always to successfully help a company build and grow its business. You do all you can to make them successful. It is also important in any campaign that your client feels you have become partners with them in business – not in public relations – in business! They should feel they cannot perform without you, that you are so important the CEO can't do without you.

Always be accessible with and for the client and always tell the truth. If you have integrity, you might not get in a story the first or second time, but you become so accessible and so important as a source of help to a journalist that you shortly become someone they rely on. Later, you will see yourself being written up a lot because you are a company that talks. When you have a problem, you admit you have a problem, and you don't let the lawyers run all over everything and direct what's being communicated.

If a client's budget is tight, segmented work to one medium – one newspaper, magazine, radio outlet, or TV network – is often the best approach. That way that medium knows that little piece is theirs alone. However, anybody who writes a lot of news releases ought to be shot, because they are not read, even if they are written well. They are usually dropped. A quick memo or phone call can be very effective. Sometimes people use e-mail as a means of avoidance because they are afraid to talk to the media. You need to become the media person's friend.

When I was dealing with the media a lot, I would first work on building a great relationship and becoming a good source. With this approach you get a lot of exposure. We would be in the news one way or another every other week because we became good sources. We would work with the media people one-on-one, as opposed to taking a shotgun approach. These days people often send releases out all over the landscape, only to find later there is precious little return for that kind of work.

I have not seen a client with a very large public relations budget in a long time. At the high end you can, of course, do a lot more, but you still have to be specific about what you are trying to do. Ask the client: What can we help you do? It should not all be publicity. If a client has a lot of money, do a great media mix. That is not abdicating the role of advertising; good public relations people should recognize what advertising can do. In advertising you can keep control. For example, if I hang my shingle on a stadium, I know it is going to look exactly the way I want it, because I paid for it to be that way. But when you go into the ether of some of the aspects of public relations such as publicity, you never quite know what is going to happen.

So if a client came to me with a large budget, I would have many elements in the campaign, but they would all strategically mesh together. Too many public relations people think publicity is the only way to go. It is just one element of what we do, and it is the element we have the least control over; but it can have a great impact if it works.

Measuring return on investment is simpler than most people realize. When you work in marketing, you are trying to sell a company's products. If a company introduces a new product line, and the PR techniques have helped that product launch and made the product name a household word, then we have done our job. If the product fails, it could be that the product is not good enough, but it could also be that the campaign was no good, and there was not enough energy or money behind the campaign.

The tactical public relations people will tell you the only way to measure the value of a campaign is the number of clippings, or the number of television and radio appearances, and I think that's all grand. But if that is your approach, then you fail to be a business partner with your client. You are trying to move his products, which increases revenue, which helps the profit line, which helps the shareholders. It is so simple. But a lot of people in PR do not want to even think that way.

Success cannot always be measured by lineage in newspapers; one article in one place may do a lot more than a bushel basket of clippings. The real purpose of what we do is to help a client sell something: a product, a service, or the client's position on an important issue. Often public relations people get mired in areas that seem standard and tactical – not strategic. If you can become a strategic partner with your client, you will have a long-term client and a long-term friend.

Think as a business person more than a public relations person. Think as your clients need to think and absorb everything you possibly can about your client's business.

Stop fiddling with tactical issues. Tactics are important, but we should start not thinking just as communicators, and start thinking primarily as business people. You may never know more than the client knows about his or her own business, but you should try to know almost as much.

Straight Talk About Individual Success

Curiosity and deep sensitivity are very important in public relations. It is all too easy to be callous and say to yourself, "We'll just do it and take the money." There is greater importance to what we do in public relations. Practiced at its highest level, public relations can be the best business in the world. Practiced at its lowest level, it is the worst business in the world.

A good public relations professional has to have high energy and think positively. When you get up in the morning, no matter what you are enshrouded with, you have to look at it from a positive point of view. When you are with a client who is demoralized about what is going on around them – perhaps their sales are down, or their reputation has been branded in a negative way – you have to stay steady. Never get too high or too low. I believe nothing good has ever come out of negative thinking. If the public relations person starts grousing with the client, then all you have are two people who are unhappy.

A PR person also needs to have a sense of humor to keep them going. Public relations these days can be all too serious. PR people take themselves too seriously and do not see that there is humor everywhere they look. With humor, you can lighten up the client and lighten up yourself.

You can be an outstanding public relations person without any true formal education, if you read a lot. When I first joined the field of public relations, virtually no one who was my senior had graduated from college, but they were brilliant writers and voracious readers. People in our field are not reading anymore, as far as I can tell. I ask people "What do you read?" They say "I read *Newsweek*." But they have not read Proust; they have not read Voltaire; they have not read about history. Public relations people could learn a lot by reading the sayings and methods of Harry Truman, for example, or the brilliance of Churchill. These days you go to a resort, and everybody is reading the same John Grisham book. That is agonizing for me – I want to be totally different from the pack.

Never lie to a client. If the agency makes a mistake, tell the client. It is better for him to find out right away, not two months later. You may sometimes feel that the client is doing the wrong thing: They may not be imbuing their audiences with the right messages, or they may be manipulating the truth. You have to tell the client they cannot do it that way, because their integrity and their reputation stand on it. There may be times when you have serious arguments with clients, when you really feel you have to tell the truth and give your opinion. That is what a counselor does. A counselor is not a yes man. A counselor is a thinker who helps a leader and sometimes says, "No, that's not the right thing to do." Truthfulness is one of the most important qualities a great public relations person can have. Do not be afraid to tell the truth, and do not be afraid to employ your thoughts. We sometimes don't realize we have the right to speak our minds and work with the clients. You don't always have to argue; just tell the client what you think is the proper way to go. That is first and foremost in any relationship. Most importantly, don't ever lie to the media. Never! If you do, it will come back to haunt you. Someone will find out, and it will create havoc for you and your client.

Don't get too far down, and don't get too far up; leadership means you stay steady in bad times and good times. Go out and meet other business people, not just public relations people.

Read about your industry. Read all the major business journals, and at least read the front page of *The Wall Street Journal,* so you know what's ticking, so you think as a businessperson. Above all, read anything you can get your hands on. Read the stuff that has stood and will stand the test of time – Hemingway, Faulkner, or some of the English writers – because it can make you a better thinker and a better writer. One becomes a good writer from good

117

reading, though at the same time, writing is a talent, like being able to play the piano. If you are not a good writer, you should go into some other business, such as commercial insurance, and you may earn a lot more money.

I have always said that the smart man makes the most amount of money in the least amount of time. I know people who think they should work 16 hours a day. If you are making only $100,000 working sixteen hours a day, you are being foolish. Moreover, it is very important to have a part of your life that is not just about the work process. If work is all you do, you are not seeing what is going on out there in America or the rest of the world. In some ways we get too much information; in other ways we do not know how to relax and spend time with our friends and family, our dogs and cats. Take up hobbies, read, get a boat. Do something that is not what you normally do – it opens the mind to other ideas.

So above all, tell the truth, be energetic, and be very curious. Telling the truth to anybody you deal with in our business is important because it shows you have integrity and wins you respect. That is very important. Having a lot of energy means you don't get depressed about things that are going badly. The more energy you use, the more energy you will obtain. There are energetic people and people who drain energy. Stay away from people who drain energy. Finally, be very curious. Be nosy. Think as a reporter does, always wanting to know everything about everything. That will make you a much better counselor.

Elevating Perceptions for a Better Future

For years on my tax form, I would write my occupation as "salesman" instead of my company title. Even though their salaries may be low, salesman make the most money in the world. In the future, I would like to see public relations salaries lowered, but with some kind of commission system based on the ability of the person to be effective for their company or client. I am not suggesting that if you get placement in *Forbes* magazine, you or your agency should get extra money. I am saying we should base our work on intensifying the corporation's revenue.

When Ross Perot worked for IBM as a salesman, he would sell out his block of work by the end of January, and every year he made more money than the CEO. Public relations people are not paid enough, and I think they could get paid a lot more if their salaries were based on what they actually contribute to a company's business. We need to be more entrepreneurial in public relations. We think too much as service providers, not thinkers. We are the concierges of business. That is very unfortunate.

Edward Bernaise is a good example of the right way to practice PR. In 1960 the hat business went down the drain because John F. Kennedy refused to wear a hat at his inauguration ceremony, which all preceding presidents had done. After a few years, the hat industry council went to Bernaise and asked him what they could do to enhance their business. He said, "Well, I have an idea, but you have to pay me $75,000 for that idea. I can give it to you in two seconds, but I want a check up front." So they gave him a check, and he told them to develop the idea among the public that it is cool to wear hats by featuring billboards of black men wearing hats. His idea worked, and hat sales went up like crazy nationwide. Bernaise always got paid up front for ideas; I think that is how the public relations business should work.

Public relations has changed so much over the years I've been involved in it, and I suspect that it will keep changing. In the future the counselor will become more important. If we are careful, we can elevate the profile and perceived value of public relations to clients. You should be so important that the CEO needs you, not just the director of communication. And if you are the director of communication, you should have an open door with the CEO. You achieve that by not thinking you are in the middle. We need to stop thinking so small and start thinking bigger. My attitude is: I would rather fail thinking big than succeed thinking small.

The more senior you become in an agency, the more senior the people you deal with in a company should be. Right now there is a ceiling. We also need to attract the best talent – many of the best people now go to other professions. One of the reasons is the public relations field does not pay enough, though it is a wonderful field if you look at the bigger picture. Many public relations people now in the corporations and agencies are being paid very well, but they would be paid better if they were at the top of the company. Very rarely have we seen a public relations officer rise to be CEO. I hope to see this happen in the future.

Ronald Watt is chairman and chief executive officer of Watt/Fleishman-Hillard, Cleveland (formerly Watt Roop & Co.), and is a nationally recognized communication counselor, marketing strategist, and creative consultant, with 35 years of experience in these fields. Mr. Watt is a member of the Arthur Page Society, an organization of senior communication professionals worldwide. He also is a member of the College of Fellows of Public Relations Society of America. He was elected to the Cleveland Advertising Association's Hall of Fame in 1999, joining only 70 other practitioners of advertising and public relations in the 100-year-history of the CAA, the nation's second largest and second oldest such organization.

Mr. Watt began his career in 1961 as a newspaper reporter for the Sun Newspapers and from 1963 to 1965 was a broadcast journalist with Storer Broadcasting stations. In

1966, he became director of public relations for the Toledo-Lucas County Port Authority and, in 1968, began his agency career at Flournoy & Gibbs. From there, he moved in 1973 to Edward Howard & Co., an affiliate of Hill & Knowlton Inc., where he served as a vice president. Mr. Watt next co-founded Watt-Jayme Public Relations in 1979, and in 1981, founded Watt, Roop & Co. – now Watt/Fleishman-Hillard.

Clients with whom Mr. Watt has worked over the years read like a "who's who" of international industry and commerce and include General Electric, Owens-Corning Fiberglas, TRW, IBM, Citicorp, NCR, Bayer USA, BP America, AT&T, Federal Express, American Express, North American Philips, Interbank/Mastercard, Marconi, University Hospitals, the Cleveland Browns and Cleveland Indians, Warner & Swasey, Allen-Bradley, Cablevision, American Industrial Hygiene Association, ABC Television, and BF Goodrich.

Accredited by the Public Relations Society of America (PRSA), Watt is past chairman of the Executive Committee of PRSA's 1,200-member worldwide Counselors Academy (1993) and from 1988 to 1991, chaired its Committee on Business Practices and Professional Standards. He also is a past president of the Greater Cleveland Chapter of PRSA (1981). Mr. Watt was a long-time director of the National Media Conference in New York City and former director of the National Conference of Christians & Jews. He served on the Visiting Committee of the College of Urban Affairs at Cleveland State University. He is a 1988 graduate of Leadership Cleveland. He also is a former director of the Citizens League.

In 1984, Mr. Watt was honored by his peers as recipient of the distinguished PRSA Lighthouse Award. He is listed in Who's Who in the World. He is a graduate of Bowling Green State University. He is also an alumnus of the Columbia University Graduate School of Business' Strategic Leadership programs. Mr. Watt has an extensive career as a jazz pianist as an avocation and vocation and has performed in clubs and concert halls throughout America, Canada, Europe, and South America.

He is the author of two books, Dateline: Ubi, a novel, and A Love Story for Cleveland, an anthology of recollections.

.

THE POWER OF PUBLIC RELATIONS IN A COMPLEX WORLD

RICHARD EDELMAN
Edelman PR Worldwide
President and Chief Executive Officer

PR as Protective Coating

Many outside our industry mistakenly believe that public relations means simply working with the press. We actually transmit clients' messages to multiple stakeholder groups in a highly complex and breathtakingly fast environment. Especially over the last decade, public relations is used in the marketing mix to create a favorable context and receptive audience that helps advertising be most effective.

We have become an essential part of corporate reputation management by attracting investors and employees, while establishing a protective coating in the event of crisis. In short, public relations is the communications technique best suited to the times, working across time zones and cultures, with speed, dialogue, and credibility.

Democratization of Communication

The traditional hierarchy of media is evolving away from dominance by "elite" print publications, such as *The Wall Street Journal* and *The New York Times* or the Big Three Networks (ABC, CBS, NBC). Cable broadcasters, such as CNN and Fox, or mass print media, such as *USA Today* are on the rise. The 24-hour news cycle, the immediacy of reporting, and the short attention span of consumers are also leading to increased use of news Web sites, most often those linked to broadcasters, such as MSNBC.com and

CNN.com. The rise of the individual investor has allowed broadcast business media, such as CNBC to become important voices, along with business publications such as *Business Week, Fortune* and *Forbes.*

Statistics tell the story of fundamental changes taking place in the media landscape. In the past decade in the U.S., viewing of major television networks during the prime time period is down from 40 percent to 25 percent of total households. Viewing of cable networks is up from 5 percent to 30 percent. The Internet is television's newest competition. Approximately 115 million Americans are now online. The average user is online 17 times a month for 19-minute sessions, splitting time among nine sites. About 36 percent of users are online at least five hours a week. Forty percent of the people online are women. Of regular Internet users, 33 percent spend less time reading newspapers than before, and 60 percent have reduced their television viewing time.

Apart from the Web, dramatic changes have taken place in every segment of the media environment with the introduction of global television networks and international editions of publications. With vertical integration of media (NBC plus MSNBC plus CNBC plus Super Channel), there is repurposing of information so it can be used across different platforms. Audiences widely dispersed throughout the world receive news immediately, but they interpret events and messages through their own cultural context.

127

They are also extremely segmented. Years ago, monthly magazines began targeting specific interest groups by age, race, lifestyle, profession, and special interest. This same segmentation is now evident in all media, with cable television best filling the need for targeted programs.

Though they have access to more information than before, audiences tend to have a narrower scope of interests. We are no longer "grazing," but instead are "cherry-picking" or narrowcasting to cope with a surfeit of information. Increasingly, information is now delivered to end users based on their past behavior or on an "as requested" basis. People get health advice customized to their age and condition. Stock tips match their interests and risk acceptance. Book reviews are delivered based on past purchases. National newsmagazines offer local editions that contain localized editorial and advertising content.

The importance of public relations has increased with the democratization of communications. Messages are being circulated directly to consumers, and responses are being received in equal measure due to the explosion of the Internet. Because computers have made two-way communication so much easier, consumers expect interactivity with all other media, as well. For instance, television talk shows now take calls and e-mails from viewers ("Larry King Live" and "Talk Back" on CNN, for example). And sports news and entertainment programming have become interactive with instant Web-based polling. There is now an expectation of instantaneous communication, with depth and context.

The most significant change of all, however, is convergence – a collision of news, entertainment, dialogue, and personal action – resulting in an average consumer having 2,000 impressions per day, as much as a person had in a lifetime only a century ago. Consumers of information now triangulate to find truth, as there is no single source of unimpeachable credibility. They build webs of trust to test their beliefs with friends and experts.

Pinging Messages Inside a Circle of Cross-Influence

The Internet and the new technology have had two major effects on the public relations industry. First, we now can communicate directly with end-users of information, as opposed to relying exclusively on the media. Second, rapid communications technology has made it much more perilous for companies who give one message to one audience and a conflicting one to another. If you just talk to Wall Street, analysts' comments will quickly find their way to regulators or to opposition groups, like NGOs (non-governmental organizations). Companies are discovering the "paradox of transparency," with greater support generated by open admission of gaps in research or flaws in product safety, as long as a path toward solution is offered.

The consumer is empowered and skeptical, holding the brand responsible for corporate behavior as never before.

A concept used to describe effective communication in the past was the "pyramid of influence." In this old model, opinion leaders received top priority, and information "trickled down" to the consumer. This model relied on elite media delivering messages in editorial form to those at the top of the pyramid. Advertising was then used to inform the mass audience and stimulate purchase.

To be effective in the age of the Internet, however, communications must be based on the "circle of cross-influence." It recognizes the importance of communicating with stakeholders positioned at every point around the edge of the sphere, each of whom influences the others. Key stakeholders now include regulators, NGOs, media, analysts, customers, retailers, employees, and academics. Within this circle, a company's messages "ping," or bounce from stakeholder to stakeholder. Consumers must be seen as a primary audience from the inception of a concept. This creates a fast-moving, unpredictable situation in which control of the message can easily be lost.

PR professionals understand this "pinging" environment created by multiple stakeholders. They know information must go out simultaneously to all audiences, using a unified set of messages. For this reason, public relations is precisely positioned to shape the dialogue in a new media environment. At the same time, it also dramatically affects the way we must practice public relations and the way it is viewed in relation to other marketing disciplines, such as advertising.

PR: A Clear Winner Over Advertising

Public relations has a unique advantage over advertising in dealing with complex issues. Advertising is a one-way street; PR deals in dialogue, speed, and credibility.

In the 50 years between the end of World War II and 1996, there were relatively few but highly developed media outlets. During that time it was possible to reach 97 percent of your target group with three TV advertisements during prime time. Today you need 45 ad exposures to achieve the same reach. During prime time, more people are watching specialized cable stations, such as ESPN, The History Channel, and the Food Channel, than the larger networks. After decades of developing one concept to reach a single mass audience, advertisers now face the problem of having to develop different but interrelated concepts to address numerous smaller target groups.

Advertising is like driving a sedan on a superhighway. Public relations is an SUV that can go off-road and adapt to various kinds of driving conditions very quickly. That adaptability is essential in today's minute-by-minute communications world, where people issue challenges on the Internet that are not always substantively based.

For more complex products, a message wrapped in a 30-second commercial is not sufficient to get a consumer to act. A technology product, for instance, can hardly be sold that way. For this reason, technology and pharmaceutical manufacturers are spending a high percentage of their marketing budget on public relations. The simpler marketing propositions – toothpaste, shaving cream, or soap – will continue to rely on advertising to focus on PR. In the long run, the more complex, expensive products will have to change their marketing mix.

Advertising should follow public relations on products that claim true health benefit or technological advantage. Advertising works very well using simple, associative, and repeatable messages. However, before you get to the emotion of buying a car, you must already have determined whether the car is durable and safe, what driving qualities it has, and how responsible the manufacturer is in the community. Public relations can build credibility via third-party testimonials. It can deliver the context and opportunity for dialogue. Public relations should be seen as a long-term commitment to engaging all publics throughout the product life cycle.

Public relations may never completely replace advertising, but PR is now assigned the crucial role of creating permission to buy. Advertising may be more comfortable to many marketing executives, but public relations is now necessary for ubiquity of message, as well as credibility. Public relations delivers complex content that is newsworthy, revealing, and persuasive. It draws on expert third parties who can define the issue in a textured manner, with nuance and sophistication.

Public relations can forge the base of support for a brand. It can clear the way for mass advertising to generate pull. It can create a multi-dimensional impression for the company marketing a product, giving people a certain sense that the company has style, intelligence, and integrity. As written in *The Economist* magazine, "Brands of the future will have to stand not only for product quality and a desirable image. They will also have to signal something wholesome about the company behind the brand."

Yo Quiero CSR

A recent study by the Prince of Wales International Business Leaders' Forum showed consumers are more willing to purchase products from companies they respect. Research by our own firm indicates corporate social responsibility (CSR) gives companies a shield in crisis and a real advantage with regulators. The key component in social responsibility is not philanthropy, but ethical conduct. A company cannot "buy it"; it has to "be it."

Other essential elements of CSR include employee relations and environmental standards. Major companies, such as Shell and BP have recognized the value of incorporating CSR into their entire business platform, including the chain of custody in production and ethical behavior by employees.

According to Howard Schultz, chairman and founder of Starbucks, "To build trust and confidence among our people, it is important that they recognize that this is a company with a conscience. We encourage people to be involved in their local communities. We also do things such as pay more than the asking price for coffee beans. That way we can get the money back into the hands of the people who grow it, often in poor countries. We don't do these things when the cameras are on. We do them all the time." Brands such as Starbucks have been created by PR and sustained by distinctive values.

We believe in the power of a simple event that has tremendous visual impact. However, a strong public relations campaign has to offer real substance and redeeming quality. The Benetton campaign met that criterion. Several years ago, for Benetton France on National AIDS Day, we worked with activists from ACT-UP to put a large pink cloth over the obelisk in the Place de la Concorde in Paris before the morning rush hour. From a distance it looked like a giant condom. This image was broadcast around the world, helping to tie the Benetton brand to AIDS awareness and prevention.

Being innovative is partly a matter of reflecting societal trends, while being edgy enough to grab media attention. Taco Bell was introducing a new tortilla chip and wanted to make a big splash. We registered an Internet site called newchips.com and let people believe there was going to be an IPO of a hot new semiconductor chip company, primarily by sending out e-mail messages to technology investor chat rooms. Two weeks later we held an event where we unveiled the new chips in Times Square, in front of the NASDAQ sign, with the Chihuahua. We gave free chips to the Wall Street traders, and we put a message up on the Web site saying, "Gotcha, sorry it's a big spoof. But by the way if you want a coupon..." We did the whole program for under $100,000, but we got results because we showed both a sense of humor and an understanding of a prevailing sensibility of the time.

Changes on the PR Horizon

There are four golden rules in public relations. The first is you absolutely cannot spin: You cannot tell half-truths and try to overly massage your story. Second, you have to establish specific and long-term relationships with reporters. Third, you have to have truly credible sources of third-party support for your position, and disclose any financial interest they may have. Finally, you have to be quick; you have to respond to opponents and not let lies go unchallenged. These rules haven't changed, but public relations will have to evolve substantially in the years ahead.

There is much greater diversity of media now. The media are highly focused on speed-to-market, so broadcast often leads the tone of the coverage. You have to counter rumors very quickly, and supply pictures for anything you do. Additionally, more power is concentrated in opposition groups, such as NGOs, which understand the power of simple stories told through pictures. Our research on NGOs in five countries indicates that NGOs enjoy a four-to-one advantage in credibility over companies, government, and media on issues of environment and health. They are truly the new global super-brands. Relationships should be forged with NGOs and other critics in advance of a public issue where both sides are posturing for effect.

Another change involves the quality of information. Reporters' sources now include chat rooms, newsgroups, and other non-traditional references. Information, especially if it is salacious, spreads more quickly than a virus. The pressure to publish stories immediately has changed journalistic standards for some in the media. Speed-to-market is a primary concern. The vertically integrated media magnify the impact of sensational material. A story will break online, and more detailed information will follow in print media. Erroneous stories are later corrected, so the stories are "works in progress."

PR professionals need to be even more vigilant in monitoring these non-traditional outlets and in checking the accuracy of their writing because information originally intended for the media is going directly to the end-user. Material posted on PR Newswire is now taken as gospel by investors and other constituents. As such, we must aim for publisher-level standards, issuing material good enough to appear in a major daily newspaper. In addition, we should provide information that is authoritative, based on sources that allow readers to check further on a story. We should offer links to third parties who are sources of our information, so peak dialogue is established.

In the future, public relations also must deliver truly global service. Global business and global media will force that change. There is one caveat: The local office doing the work must have the right to adapt the creative approach to suit local tastes. Companies are becoming increasingly aware of the importance of public relations in an international market. Consider the study we did a couple of years ago on the Bridgestone tire situation. We found that an American spokesman for Bridgestone would have been far more credible than a Japanese spokesman in the United States. Conversely, when American companies go overseas, they must accept the premise that their products are a proxy for America. Companies are beginning to understand this and are increasingly sourcing their raw materials from the local markets, trying to build community ties. They recognize that they must be much more than marketers in a non-U.S. context, that brand is morphing with corporate reputation.

Compensation: A Struggle for Validation

One of the biggest challenges in public relations is overcoming questions about the size of budgets. We are past the point where people wonder whether they need public relations at all. Most now accept the fact that public relations is essential but may not appreciate the cost of quality. We have to continue to pay increasingly higher salaries to get smart, nimble people who have specific industry expertise and also have an ability to work in other professions. To get the best people, we have to keep pace with salaries in finance, investment banking, law, and other fields. As a result, the struggle is the new price point.

The compensation structure in public relations should change. We may be moving toward evaluation on the basis of product movement, change in awareness, or improved corporate reputation. These are preferable to other indicators, such as ad equivalency, where somebody says, "Well, we had X number of people read this, and this space is worth $2.50 per clipping..." This is superficial and simplistic, an inappropriate reduction of the power of PR in providing credibility and content.

Right now compensation is cost-based; in other words, our fees are the cost of the hours spent, based on the salaries of the practitioners. That is fine, but a success criterion should also be included in the mix. We sometimes have a very disproportionate effect on the outcome of a business situation, whether it is in mergers and acquisitions or in a product launch. There is precedent here among other professionals; lawyers get success fees, and public relations people should consider this structure, too.

The Opportunity for Public Relations

For the first time, public relations can compete on level ground with advertising for investment in marketing and reputation management. *Brandweek* recently noted, "Public relations has taken on a whole new role in brand building... This technique of influencing the influencer, heavily used by technology companies, is now finding its way into the marketing of ordinary consumer companies. The technique works well with the skeptical consumer in an information-rich society."

A primary value of public relations is its dynamic quality and credibility in a complex world. As business globalizes, public relations must adapt to capitalize. PR people must recognize the "circle of cross-influence." They must expand their knowledge of the new stakeholders, such as NGOs, and investigate every possible means of communicating with them. PR professionals must assure substantive, factual content to ensure acceptance of material by end users. Given a continuously improved offering, we have the ability to become the primary communications methodology for the complex business issues coming in the years ahead.

Richard Edelman was named president and chief executive officer, Edelman Public Relations Worldwide in September 1996. Before that, he served as president of Edelman Public Relations, U.S. operations, regional manager, Europe, and manager of the New York office of the firm.

Mr. Edelman has extensive experience in marketing, with current assignments for American Home Products and FujiFilm. He has particular interest in the technology and media areas, where he has worked for Bertelsmann, Time Warner, and Viacom. He has advised global firms on financial relations, including the recent New York Stock Exchange listing of VEBA, the fourth largest company in Germany. He managed the communications for the "deal of the year" in 1994, the merger of Viacom, Blockbuster, and Paramount, and assisted Deutsche Bank on its 1999 acquisition of Bankers Trust. He has assisted several countries on economic development programs, including Egypt, Israel, and Mexico.

Mr. Edelman won the Silver Anvil, the highest award in the public relations industry, in 1981. He was named "Best Manager of the Year" by Inside PR magazine in 1995.

Serving on the boards of directors of the New York Historical Society and Centers for Disease Control Foundation, Mr. Edelman is also a member of the World Economic Forum, the Arthur Page Society, and PR Seminar. He has worked on several political campaigns, including Jim Thompson for Governor and Ed Koch for Mayor.

Mr. Edelman graduated from Phillips Exeter Academy in 1972. He has a Bachelor of Arts degree from Harvard College and an MBA from Harvard Business School.

SUCCESS IN PUBLIC RELATIONS

LOU RENA HAMMOND
Lou Hammond & Associates
Founder and President

The State of PR

The art of public relations is one of influencing public opinion. It relies on our ability to identify clear goals, think strategically, and display impeccable judgment in developing and implementing our plans. First and foremost, we must have an intimate knowledge of our clients' businesses – and of their customers, their employees, and their shareholders. Only then can we truly understand what approaches will be effective in our public relations efforts and which audiences we need to reach. Knowing the audience is key. We must continuously ask ourselves: Who are we trying to reach?

The acceptance of public relations as a business, a trade, and a service that can bring results and affect the bottom line is a relatively new phenomenon. There was a time when we in public relations were called "publicists," and our profession was on the fringes of key business priorities. Today that has changed. Virtually all organizations now consider public relations vital to their success and have a greater appreciation of what public relations efforts can achieve. When we do encounter a misunderstanding of the profession, it tends to be with people who have difficulty distinguishing between the practices of public relations and advertising. Those who have not previously used public relations in their business plans have a tendency to blur the line between the two.

Technology has had an enormous impact on our business. Today, everything is instantaneous and 24/7. And while I strongly believe the benefits of this new age far outweigh the negatives, it does present some new issues for public relations practitioners. For instance, when reporters decide to write about a topic, a quick search on the Internet can take them back decades, providing in-depth, long-term background on the subject. This keeps us on our toes. We must have as much knowledge about the topic as the reporters we are trying to help.

The continuous, instantaneous nature of the news is also changing our business. Today's public relations practitioners must be ready to respond to a development within at least the same news cycle – and preferably within the hour – or risk seeing their message muffled, even lost, in our "all news, all the time" mind-set.

While we are certain to see technology continuing to change the practice of public relations, let's not forget the importance of the warm handshake and the face-to-face meeting. No matter how powerful the Internet or how rapid e-mail delivery, our business is about relationships.

I'm very optimistic about the future of our profession. The more widespread acceptance and understanding of public relations has led to more emphasis being placed on these disciplines in our colleges and universities. This will lead to an even greater number of bright, young, and talented individuals wanting to enter the field. At a time when we are all conscious of the changing economy, I maintain the public relations business is among the more "recession-proof" sectors of today's business landscape. While a client's advertising budget may be cut, public relations often remains because it offers a more economical solution for communications implementation.

Driving for Success in Public Relations

To be successful, every public relations strategy must be centered on the brand. The power of a brand can never be underestimated. It is the role of public relations to enhance and strengthen it. The brand becomes the essence of what we are trying to communicate. Our strategies must be based on a deep understanding of this valuable asset, the inspiration behind it, and the leverage it holds. This means having an equally good understanding of the audiences we are trying to reach.

The brand and what it stands for must also be paramount in our thinking as we develop tactics to implement our strategies. This is why we make every effort to stay close to our clients, meeting frequently to discuss developments that might affect the messages and communication tools we are using. To have a strong and lasting relationship, we must be realistic with clients, never over-promising – "under-promise and over-service," I like to say – and making certain we are in agreement on strategy and the results expected.

We work to find a message that will get attention: What does this client do that is different and exciting, and that sets them apart from others in their field? Then the key is to direct the message to the right people and present it in such a way that it gets their attention. For some clients, media relations activities will be deemed the best approach, while with others we may determine that events and promotions are the more effective means of communicating. Most often we'll use a combination of both, in which case we must be certain that all the aspects of the program are well coordinated, so one adds value to the other.

In media relations, we work hard at being innovative, creating programs that are designed specifically for each client. We emphasize good writing and targeting the right media for the story or the product; and we pride ourselves on creating high-quality materials, from press kit covers to photographs and video.

As with media relations work, events and promotions must be in keeping with the brand image. The theme, the location, the invitees, and the amenities must all reflect the brand and serve to support it. Larger is not always better. In fact, we believe that smaller events, where the media and guests have an opportunity to meet personally with our clients, offer the most beneficial results.

Innovation is key to the success of public relations. It shows itself not only in the way a program or event is handled, but in other, less obvious ways as well. Our agency does things differently. For instance, we maintain our own 30,000-name mailing list in-house. As we own the list, we keep it updated and categorized on an ongoing basis, making it available on a moment's notice. We are also different in the way we have developed our Web site. Our site is designed for use by the media, whom we consider to be our company's primary audience. The site is not about us; it is about our clients. Reporters find it useful, and our clients see it as added value.

It is hard to measure return on investment in public relations. We can determine the value of press clippings in terms of advertising and find impressive results. We can also judge a campaign's success by determining whether sales and phone volume increased and goods moved off the shelf at a faster rate. Or we can use a more targeted approach by encouraging use of a designated 800 number for consumer information, thereby learning not only of the interest that a campaign may have created, but also its effect on driving sales. The true measure of return on investment, however, remains elusive. How can we measure our relationships with the media? How can we measure awareness that may pay off in the long run, in a year or two? These questions are hard to answer and always will be.

While it is always difficult to measure success, one significant measurement for an agency is client retention. We have a number of clients who have been with us for more than a decade, and a quarter of our clients have been with us more than five years. Our new business comes from referrals by clients and the media, and I consider that to be a strong indication of success. If our clients are happy, if they renew their contracts, and if we are targeting and meeting their needs, then we are succeeding. With success comes growth, and I believe we need to maintain a limited growth rate to allow us to continue to give the kind of service expected from us and for which we have gained a reputation.

Succeeding in PR as an Individual

To succeed in public relations, you must be creative, committed to hard work, and gracious under stress. A practitioner must have organizational skills in handling diverse assignments, often several at a time. Excellent writing skills and self-expression are indispensable tools when entering the profession.

At the agency level, enthusiasm is essential. You can help employees become better writers; you can teach them the principles of public relations; but you cannot teach enthusiasm. Either a person has it, or they don't. We look for people with a can-do attitude.

Finally, you must be optimistic and, at the same time, honest and realistic. Your relationship with clients, as with colleagues and employees, is built on trust. Be fair. Be upfront and totally truthful about what can be delivered. All of this leads to long-term client and employee loyalty – in my opinion the true measure of success in any business.

As founder and president of Lou Hammond & Associates, Lou Rena Hammond has transformed a three-employee, three-client company into an award-winning independent marketing communications agency with 35 employees and more than 30 prestigious clients. Over the past 16 years, she has led the agency in its service of clients through public relations, public affairs, international promotions, product introductions, and crisis communications.

Ms. Hammond earned national recognition as winner of the 1992 Matrix Award for public relations from Women in Communications, Inc. Other personal and corporate honors include the 1994 Creativity in Public Relations Award (CIPRA) from Inside PR; the Public Relations Society of America's 1991, 1994, and 1995 Big Apple Awards; the 1993 Supplier of the Year Award from client Hunter Douglas Window Fashions; the 1993 Atlas Award from the Association of Travel Marketing Executives; the 1991 Winthrop W. Grice Award from the Hospitality Sales and Marketing Association International (HSMAI); 35 HSMAI Golden Bell Awards; The Fragrance Foundation's

Award for Best Launch; and a spot on the Inside PR All-Star List.

Ms. Hammond developed her specialty in marketing to sophisticated, upscale consumers during her 15-year tenure at Pan American World Airways, where she served as director of special projects, promotion, publicity, and public affairs. Her earlier experience includes editorial assignments as calendar editor with Avenue magazine and promotional responsibilities for Dior du Liban.

THE ART AND SCIENCE OF PUBLIC RELATIONS

ANTHONY J. RUSSO, PH.D.
Noonan Russo Communications
Chief Executive Officer

PR's Evolution to Art and Science

The art of public relations is centered on our ability to understand a client's business at virtually every level. From an inside perspective, this understanding must extend beyond a knowledge of what a particular company offers in terms of products or services and into the realm of how they sell, with what types of people, using which kinds of tools. Often the answers to these questions help the PR professional select or discard specific types of strategies and tools from the outset as fitting or not fitting into the "personality" of a given client. The PR professional must also gain understanding of how a client's business intersects with other businesses, its interaction with peer groups, and how it fits into the universe of other companies performing similar functions.

The science of public relations is its tactical implementation. Given some set of facts with a defined set of communications objectives superimposed, the tactics frequently dictate themselves. Here, proven relationships determine success. Persistence does the rest.

Success can quite simply be defined as achieving or exceeding the goals that were agreed upon at the outset of a relationship. This has everything to do with becoming an extension of the client's management team, translating into an ability to shape corporate vision and not simply package it into a press release.

The Evolution of PR

The practice of public relations has become more challenging in the last decade. This has happened because of two primary factors. First, there has been an elevation of the PR function in many organizations. Effectively, this elevation facilitated the practice of PR from science only to art and science. Translated, this means there is now a seat at the boardroom table for the public relations professional. Second, there is an increased sophistication in the tools available for communication. The presence of both factors has resulted in the need for specialization within the practice of public relations. Such a need is especially evident in fields such as technology, biotechnology, and healthcare, where an intimate familiarity with the industry's landscape is key to effectively communicating on behalf of a given client or group of clients within an industry.

Once you've established the ability to speak a "common language" with a client, the bar for performance remains very high. The PR professional needs to translate the client's message to a lay audience while, at the same time, facilitating the client's efforts to continue meeting new goals and objectives. I like to compare this to visiting a foreign country. You may know the language, and that's one of the reasons you want to visit. But you also have to understand the culture, how that culture compares and contrasts to other cultures, and how to integrate cultures, when it becomes appropriate.

The Internet has affected how we practice in almost every aspect of the communications business. Central to this effect is that the Internet affords even the smallest company the opportunity to serve the global marketplace. Small companies recognize this opportunity and reach out to communications consultants earlier and earlier in the corporate life cycle to ensure they develop the tools they need to leverage the opportunity.

A good example of how this works is through the evolution of the press conference. In the past, you had to either attend the event in person or rely on broadcast media to provide access to the information discussed. The Internet offers any interested party full and unedited access to the information from anywhere in the world and in real time. Global interaction, through the use of extranets, adds the ability to communicate with the newsmaker, providing feedback in real time, as well. Essentially, this gives a company the ability to communicate messages to very specific audiences.

When we look at the Internet as a communications tool, we see a medium that has opened up the global arena, enabling companies to be agile and quick in the way they communicate with target audiences. That said, technology needs to continue its role as an industry driver in public relations, perhaps even more than in other fields. The PR professional deals with so many audiences and so many different messages; technology enables us to refine those messages and to target them to the audiences they need to reach the most. Strategic and cost effective, the use of technology fits with the implementation of public relations programs at every juncture.

The future of public relations remains bright because more and more companies are turning to the professionals for advice, for all the reasons discussed above and others. We have seen this with the anthrax scares – situations where government officials admitted not knowing what to say or how to say it. It is certain, therefore, that public relations professionals shaped most of the messages that were disseminated and discussed publicly regarding the anthrax scare. So, too, is much of what is filtered to the public regarding the fight against terror in which the United States and other countries are engaged. While the media do have the power of selectivity in choosing what stories they write about, the public relations professional is usually the gatekeeper of which choices will be offered.

Think Strategically – Putting PR to Work

The golden rule of public relations is "Think strategically and not tactically." All of the movement in the evolution of the field has been centered on this principle. We have become valued as strategic counselors, not as tacticians, and we need to continuously strive to reinforce that role with our clients. Ideally, that seat at the boardroom table has a brass plate with our name on it.

From an implementation standpoint, the first thing I do is sit down with a client to delineate their goals. I find out why a campaign is needed, what it needs to reflect in both the short and the long terms, and how that implementation should look. I also remind the client it's not just about creating a "buzz" – it's about creating the right sort of "buzz."

Ensuring the right "buzz" starts with creation of the right messages, and these stem from a company's goals and mission. Some companies are not even sure of their goals; in these cases, we start at the beginning and work our way forward. When a company does understand its goals, we work to develop appropriate messages around them and then discuss and practice the best way to articulate them in terms of a public relations plan.

Once the goals and the messages are in place, the plan itself can take many forms – from putting together a single conference to a series of events and from a press-release-only strategy to a release-conference call-webcast approach. Regardless of which form it takes, the goal is to build the campaign or series of campaigns on a solid foundation by putting together a strategic effort that will culminate in a series of events for a defined target audience or audiences. The key to success here is to understand what you want to achieve with respect to those audiences and let the campaign take root on that basis.

To ensure a solid foundation, it is imperative that the initial corporate goals be realistic and achievable and that they reflect the direction the company wants and believes it can take. The first line of strategic public relations counsel is predicated on this idea. For example, sometimes clients will say, "We just want to get into *The Wall Street Journal.* That's our goal." I reply, "That is a tactic, not a strategy. Let's talk about the realistic goals you have with the potential to result in a placement." In other words, the goal is to communicate to a prestigious target financial audience. To achieve that goal, the company must have some piece of news that would likely appeal to such an audience in the first place.

In some cases, the *Journal* isn't really the right publication to start targeting, given a client's particular stage of development. Perhaps a regional business journal is the best place to start, or local daily papers. Our job is to evaluate the goals in terms of achievable placements and to communicate this to the client at the outset, so they are not disappointed in the outcome. I spend a lot of time questioning goals and the appropriate communications vehicles to achieve them. I think it's fine for a client to come in with a pre-determined set of goals, but frequently it feels a bit like telling a surgeon what instruments he or she should use.

To help a company achieve its visibility goals, we look at many factors. These include the unique aspects of their product or product portfolio, points of differentiation from the competition, or a unique method of producing a product. We examine corporate strategy, looking to see if the company was built using an interesting business model, or, better yet, a model that's never been used before. Our job is to leverage the unique aspects of the company to establish the perception of leadership in a niche area, wherever possible. It might be a new food item from McDonald's, for example, a burger that tastes better or is more nutritious than its fast-food counterparts. Maybe it's more fun. The general idea is to identify which factors apply and use them to drive visibility for a product or service and momentum for a company.

In public relations, tools and methods of implementation vary according to available budget. Given a generous budget, we like to work first on establishing a set of good core materials. This includes putting together a Web site that can address the various audiences and communicate the company's unique points of differentiation. We think through a Web strategy that incorporates this idea, and then put programs together that truly enable the Web site to serve as a driver of corporate messages. Globalization plays a role here, too. We need to evaluate the need for a multi-lingual site, as well as ensure that the translations of Web materials are effective and do not somehow offend the local culture.

We might also facilitate the advertising process, put together conferences, hire speakers, and develop appropriate educational programs. We try to think through which tools can effectively reach our target audiences at different levels. Achieving this may also include hard-copy mailings of materials to key people, corporate attendance at trade shows and conferences, or the initiation of a full-blown advertising campaign run in conjunction with the public relations initiative.

If the budget is small, it comes down to being very focused in our program development and implementation. Selection of appropriate tools here is critical. In the small-budget scenario, we may be faced with reaching out to target audiences at one or two levels instead of four or five. Alternatively, we may initiate one mass campaign with the idea of reaching every audience with one tool and incorporating multiple target audience messages into that single effort. Success here means each target would take away the messages meant for them, and then some. Success breeds new opportunity, and when working with smaller-budget clients, we hope to "wow" them with the results, so we can initiate larger programs for them going forward.

So, Does It Work? Measuring PR Return

I think metrics, return on investment, is an area neither widely understood nor widely employed by public relations practitioners. It is, in fact, seldom part of a program unless the scope of the project is very large. However, measuring results is probably one of the most important things we can do. Tangible ROI increases client confidence, enables new opportunity in terms of creativity, and generates new business. Traditionally, results have been measured by numbers of clippings; truly, impressions set the level of the bar for a long time.

Now we conduct audits at the beginning and mid-point of a relationship, where we examine messages and how they are being perceived by target audiences. We evaluate goals (Have they changed since the program began?) and review how messages are being communicated. In essence, we have started setting the bar higher ourselves. If in the end we have a huge number of media placements we can show the client, which also reflect the messages we've created – that's great. Usually, however, a modest number of strategic placements that contain or support the company's key messages can indicate an important measure of success.

This means that in terms of ROI and evaluation of impressions, we delve into the content of each impression. The question becomes, "Are the messages, as we defined them, reflected in the placements?"

Although much of what we are discussing here relates to preparation of messages and materials for external audiences, public relations can, and usually should, contain an internal communications component. The primary goal of internal communications is to ensure that everybody at the company, not just its spokespeople, understands the company's messages and knows how to articulate them appropriately. This is especially true in the case of a public company where corporate value is, simply put, based on public perception of corporate fulfillment of the organizational mission and goals. Another important component of the internal message sell relates to how well the average employee "buys into" the company's messaging. Chances are, if the employee base doesn't buy into the positioning, neither will key external audiences.

Strategy Applied – A Biotechnology Example

A successful corporate sell, both internally and externally, is best exemplified by a small, private, German-based firm my company started working with several years ago. They came in saying they wanted visibility in the United States, but when questioned about their corporate mission and goals, they could not effectively articulate an overall strategy. When we took a careful look, what emerged was a story of a company – part biotechnology and part e-commerce – that did not fit into any single category or offer an easily identifiable leverage point from which to generate momentum.

After listening to their story a number of times, we told them to step back from the labels of biotechnology and e-commerce and accept that they were not either/or, but both. Then, we encouraged the company to embrace this duality as a point of differentiation between them and other healthcare companies. Finally, we identified a milestone, or upcoming event, that would enable us to communicate the dual positioning to key target audiences. Essentially, given that this company's primary goal was to garner visibility, we sought to leverage their positioning difference as an asset.

Once this overall strategy was in place, we evaluated the tactics and refined the messages. On this front, we looked at the firm's core competency – the development of software tools that employed molecular biology to find "druggable targets." Translated, this meant our client used IT to further the efficient development of biotechnology drugs. Did this blur the lines between traditional biotechnology and IT? Definitely, and it was this blurring of the lines that helped the company stand out regarding differentiation in terms of its overall corporate messages. It was amazing to see the change in the client. As they became comfortable with the positioning, they went from saying, "Well, we have to fit somewhere," to "IT and biotech – the basis of a whole new approach to the business."

The next step was to publicly launch the new positioning. This took the form of a milestone announcement regarding a partnership of our client's technology with a major pharmaceutical company. The news angle was two-pronged for this event. First, we concentrated on the deal, which included a large monetary payment, to justify the business and financial angles of the story. Second, we married the deal and its validation of the company's technology with the introduction of "i-biology – where IT and biotechnology meet."

Tactically, we used traditional outreach tools, including hard-copy press kits and one-on-one calls to reporters, as well as the Internet, to reach audiences around the world. We also employed an embargo strategy on a geographic basis to help ensure that key media in the U.S. and Europe could all break the story the morning the release was disseminated. The embargos enabled us to reach out to key German, British, and U.S. reporters before the day of the announcement and provide in-depth explanation of a complicated and technical topic, as well as introduce the branded i-biology terminology.

The end result included placements in major publications around the world, including the *Financial Times, The Wall Street Journal,* top-tier German publications, and leading trade publications. In fact, access to the information was so widespread that we reached beyond our specific targeted audiences to those interested in the emerging field for which we had just introduced the name. Ultimately, the client benefited not only with greater visibility, but also with the opportunity to reach the initial public offering stage of development about 12 months before expected.

From a positioning standpoint among the financial community, the field of "convergence," or the merger between IT and biotechnology, was born. As a public company today, the client is known as a pioneer in this field and still uses the branded i-biology terminology.

Finding Career Success in PR

Experience and passion for this work are the most important keys to success in a public relations career. This is a field in which you can become good by having a lot of different experiences, and those experiences help you have a sense of mission and allow you to be a good counselor to your clients.

Beyond experience, it's important to have a sense of vision for the field, to know when to use technologies, how to embrace them, and how to grow business. You have to be in tune with what other PR firms are doing, know how to build a best practice based on your own experience and the experience of others, and create a new product or a new type of product that is somehow going to offer new value.

These are the qualities and skills that make leaders in public relations.

The Excitement of PR

I still get excited over a press conference that everyone attends, a front-page article I've placed in *The New York Times*, an article that has all of the key messages we've worked on for months. Those things excite me because I see the results of my work in a newspaper, articulated at a press conference, or somehow appearing in a broadcast outlet that really reflects what I set out to say. Helping carve those messages, and then having a hand in deciding where and how those messages will unfold and to what audiences, is very exciting.

Very early in my career, when I was faced with a very difficult problem, my boss said to me, "Well, if it were easy, they wouldn't have hired a PR firm." I remember this every time I'm faced with a new challenge and try to impart the same problem/solution focus to those I work with.

PR and Mentoring – A Necessary Partnership

In most fields, entry-level professionals grow more quickly and develop a greater skills depth when they have a mentor to help guide them along. This is especially true in the field of public relations, where experience and contacts are key to the success of any practicing professional. The role of the protégé is to first gain an understanding of the kinds of skills he or she needs to learn and seek out a mentor who can impart that learning experience.

Implicit in this approach is my philosophy that it is critical for people to start the learning process at the "bottom," regardless of their background or education. The Ph.D. needs to learn the entry-level person's job before moving on to setting strategy and direct-to-client relations. In some industries it may not be critical to understand the job at every level to reach senior standing. However, in a public relations environment, which is usually fast-paced and dynamic, it is critical that the most senior member of the team know how to implement the tactical aspects of the job, even though more junior staff might ordinarily carry them out. These tactical elements include such activities as sending out a press release, drawing up media lists, and responding to routine media inquiries. Working through the levels also enables people to discover what they do best and what they would like to do better. The mentor plays a critical role in this process and can make identifying strengths and desired areas of expertise easier.

I see the role between mentor and protégée as symbiotic – an exchange of information for growth that works both ways.

As a mentor, I try to communicate many of the skills and techniques that have enabled my success over the years. Certain things are simple, while others are more complex. Overall, such factors include a focus on strategy and message development, the ability to play the devil's advocate with a smile, and techniques on how to keep from being intimidated by clients in difficult situations. I use these last two examples because, over the years, I've come to realize that young public relations professionals may find it difficult to challenge a client at the same time they come to realize the client is paying their salary. As a consultant, however, and no matter how young the executive is, it is critical to challenge the client at many junctures. In fact, it is the challenges and solutions to those challenges that we bring to the table that the client values most highly.

Anthony J. Russo is the co-founder and chief executive officer of Noonan/Russo Communications. Before establishing his own agency, he was vice president and manager of Corporate Communications of the Science and Healthcare Division of Cameron Associates, a New York City-based public relations firm.

During his career, Dr. Russo achieved remarkable success in obtaining superior quality news coverage for biopharmaceutical and healthcare service companies. He has held senior level posts at several public relations firms, including Adams & Rinehart and Gavin Anderson & Company. Earlier, he was the assistant to the chairman of Mocatta Metals Corporation, the world's largest bullion trading company. He is the recipient of the PRSA Philip Dorf Award for mentoring young public relations professionals.

Dr. Russo received a MA and a Ph.D. in psychology from Columbia University and Claremont University, respectively. He has also held research positions at Vanderbilt, Johns Hopkins, and Harvard. He graduated cum laude with a BA and departmental honors in psychology from Alfred University.

An active member of The New York Biotech Association, The Public Relations Society of America, and The American Psychology Association, Dr. Russo is a frequent speaker at industry conferences. He also serves on the board of directors of the Greater New York Chapter of the March of Dimes and is a member of the National Association of Science Writers.

CRITICAL ELEMENTS OF SUCCESS IN PUBLIC RELATIONS

THOMAS L. AMBERG
Cushman Amberg Communications
President and Chief Executive Officer

Wanted: People Who Lead People

The key elements for success in the field of public relations involve a good understanding of the principles of marketing, a thorough knowledge of the needs and requirements of news organizations, and the ability to write in a creative and forceful fashion. A person must be aggressive enough to have the ability to interact creatively with the media. As much as we like to talk about other activities within the realm of public relations, the number-one activity has always been media relations. If you can't write well, and if you can't work effectively with the media, then you will have significant problems.

Public relations is often described by people outside the industry as a profession for those who "love to work with people." Hearing that makes me cringe. Public relations is not for people who are at the low end of the chain; it is for people at the high end. It is for people who will ultimately be good consultants and good counselors for their clients. Public relations people, when they are really doing their job, have to be strong enough counselors that they can advise their clients on how to conduct their business. That isn't someone who just likes to work with people; instead, it is someone who has a firm grasp of business principles and understands communication and communication techniques and can be effective in steering a client and a client's business in the right direction. People who just want a job "working with people" need to apply to McDonalds.

The art of public relations is being perceptive enough to understand how to drive the right messages to the right audiences, using a variety of different communications techniques, the most prominent of which is media relations. You must be able to perceive and understand the nuances to be able to effectively drive those messages. It means having an intuitive feel for what the audience needs and having a good feel for what the client has that can satisfy the needs of his audiences. A good public relations practitioner is an aggressive person who not only is savvy but also understands the business of his client and what it will take to drive that business forward.

People are by far the biggest challenge in public relations. It is always a challenge to find the right people and the best people, the people who are truly educated in ways that will clearly benefit the clients. Finding these people is tough. There doesn't seem to be any one pathway into the public relations profession. We find people with journalism or communications backgrounds, legal or education backgrounds, business and economics majors, and even political science or art majors. So there are a wide variety of educational or career backgrounds that come our way. We think that's a good thing, because it gives our staff a wider view and different perspectives.

The challenge is in finding people in these fields who are intuitive thinkers, and who have a solid understanding of marketing and management issues. They have to be sharp enough to be able to analyze an issue or a situation, and then aggressive enough to be able to find solutions for the client. That may involve creativity issues in finding storylines that interest the media, or in writing persuasive copy for brochures, or organizing a company's presentation at a trade show, or a variety of other tactical elements. And it certainly involves being able to conceive strategies to drive a client's business forward. Finding people capable of doing these things is a huge challenge for all agencies.

A separate people problem often arises on the client end of things. It is tough to find clients who really understand what public relations is and how it ought to be used. Having clients who don't understand this can be a major challenge.

So it becomes very important to educate your client on the true purpose and goals of public relations. It is not a publicity machine. It should not be used simply to get ink or airtime. It is a skill that should be used very carefully to mold opinion and to get what is good or effective about an organization out to the public that needs to know about it. Public relations is an effective tool when it's used as part of an overall marketing and communications program to drive messages. It should be used as a mechanism for helping to communicate an organization's messages. It should be used to help that organization achieve its objectives. This education cycle takes place from the time you begin with a client to the point at which they really see the importance of what public relations can do. That understanding is not achieved by all clients or with all agencies, and it essentially comes through trust. The longer you work with a client, the longer that client has to understand what you do and to build trust in your judgment and in your ability to help them drive their business.

The reason education is so important is that when you start an account relationship, particularly with an organization that has never used public relations before, they often think strictly in terms of how much publicity they can get for their new product or for their company. They think you go in and get one story, and that one story will make a big and real difference for them. With education, they come to understand that public relations is not about a one-shot story. They realize it is not about a little publicity that revolves around some new gadget they have. Instead, it is all about understanding the right messages about their organization or its product. It's about getting continuity of exposure through publicity, through trade shows, through direct mail, through a variety of techniques that will continuously reinforce that client's reputation and its product's quality points. It is a long-term process.

PR and Advertising: A Powerful Alliance

Perhaps most importantly, public relations can help create credibility for a brand, something advertising simply can't do. It can also build or reinforce a reputation. While advertising can create frequency and reach, giving a product or brand greater awareness, you don't really believe in the brand based on advertising alone. Public relations can add that all important third-party endorsement that comes through news media coverage of your brand. People find credibility in what they read in the newspapers, see on TV news, or hear on the radio. Combining the awareness created by advertising with the credibility that comes from a public relations approach results in a very important dynamic working for any brand.

To be extremely general, the things that are most important in a campaign of any sort are creativity and a good strategy. A product introduction is one thing. A campaign involving corporate positioning is another. The vast differentiation of events and campaigns makes it quite hard to generalize on what makes a campaign come to life. However, creativity and good strategic direction are always essential.

Creativity does not necessarily mean creating something wild or off the wall. Instead, creativity relates to the approach to your problem. In terms of strategy, it is essential to have a good program that makes sense. There needs to be a method to what you are doing. There needs to be a plan where you know you are going first from point A to point B, and then from point B to point C. Those two things – creativity and strategic direction – are essential in any kind of public relations program. Public relations programs have to be forward-thinking and have to chart a way to drive a client's business goals. They can't be centered only in the present, even though much of the tactical work may be handling current problems.

The client largely sets the goals of a campaign. When we begin a new account, we sit down with our new client and begin by talking about their objectives and goals. What do they really need to come out of a public relations program? Very often, the initial response is simply, "Well, we need more awareness for" this or that, or "We are looking for publicity for a product introduction." It is a very shallow type of response. We then take them through a process of closely examining what their objectives are, what is reasonable and important to their organization, and how their objectives can affect each audience they need to reach. We have them help us lay out what we feel is the foundation for any good public relations program, which is a very thorough identification of the objectives, the audiences, and the messages. If we understand those three things, from there comes a good, solid public relations program.

Again, it is necessary to remember that public relations is not in competition with other marketing activities. Instead, it is most often one part of the marketing mix. Public relations and advertising supply both sides of the coin. Advertising gives you reach and frequency, and public relations gives you credibility. Public relations can help build a reputation for a product or a company. Advertising can get your most fundamental themes and messages out. They work together. Public relations has never had the ability to deliver reach and frequency; advertising can. But no amount of advertising can supply the credibility you also need and get from public relations.

The power of a public relations campaign can be enormous. A recent example may illustrate that point. My agency was approached by a coal mining company in central Illinois, which explained it had been haggling over contract performance issues with its primary customer (a large utility) for more than a year and had spent more than $2 million in legal fees to that point with no results.

Now, the coal company's president explained, the utility had sent the company a letter indicating they would no longer accept coal from the company 90 days from the date of the letter. Because the original contract had ten years left on it, the loss to the coal company would be approximately $400 million, and the loss of the utility contract would necessitate the closing of the mine and the elimination of the 225 jobs there. Was there something we could do, I was asked, to bring pressure on the utility to honor its contract?

We devised a plan to marshal the community and its political leaders to fight for the contract. We researched the economic impact the mine's closing would have on the small county where the mine was located. We created briefing books for all political leaders and met with them to make sure they understood what was at stake. We worked with the media to center the story on how the utility's unfair actions would devastate a county and the families of hundreds of miners. We organized picketing of the utility's headquarters by members of the United Mine Workers of America. And we organized the largest rally ever held in the county, bringing in a United States Senator and virtually every political leader representing the area to demand the utility reverse its action.

Four days after the rally, the utility caved in and said it would honor its contract with the mine. The power and force of a public relations campaign had achieved the primary goal of saving the contract, and in doing so had saved many people's jobs and averted a crippling economic blow to a small county. No amount of advertising, direct mail, or any other marketing activity could have accomplished the same thing in so short a time.

Making a Campaign Work

So many people and companies compete with the media today for so many products and services. A huge flow of information is directed to the media, seeking to create greater awareness for various products and companies and services. The only way you can distinguish them and make one stand out from another – and get them onto a short list for the media – is by having a real knowledge of the product itself and the company, as well as a real understanding of the media you are dealing with. Reporters can tell very easily if the person they are talking to doesn't really understand the industry or the product itself.

Likewise, in trying to gain greater awareness for a product or a service, if I arbitrarily start working with media, regardless of whether that media person might actually be covering the kinds of things I am trying to encourage him to, I am not going to get very far. I will instead spend most of my time talking to the wrong people. You must understand who you are talking to and whether they are genuinely interested in what you are telling them. Does the PR person know the media? Does he or she understand them and how they work? Does he know what the publication has written about in the past? Does he know what the individual reporter has written about? If you have this knowledge, then you can approach the reporter. You can then give them a customized story, tailored to fit their specific needs. Public relations is not one-size-fits-all.

When you have a large budget to work with, things tend to be more fun, a little more interesting, and a little splashier. However, a larger budget does not make these things any more important. You can do things with big events, with more sponsorship. These things get noticed. They are productive, and they are fun for the staff to deal with. But with a small client, the only tool in your toolbox might be working with the media, which can also be very productive. Generally, you go up the scale from media relations, which is a fundamental for most public relations campaigns, and as you start adding more money to it, you start getting into things such as trade show representation, events, sponsorships, media tours, and satellite media tours. You can use a variety of different tools, all of which are interesting, and all of which have the same goal, which is to help you drive a specific message to a specific audience using the media as the channel to get to that audience.

Either way, to create a successful campaign, you must be innovative. You must be able to understand the client's business and the client's industry, all the while looking for new ways to get onto people's radar screens. Being innovative doesn't necessarily mean having the latest gadgetry or the latest software. It means being the most creative. It means knowing new and better ways to get the message across to any of the audiences you need to reach. That type of innovation comes from having the right people, because when you get right down to it, public relations is still about having the right people, not just the right tools.

Lastly, to have a successful firm, not just a successful campaign, a few things must be avoided at all times. First of all, never lie to the media. If you do, the media will never forgive you, and you and your agency will have a destroyed reputation. Secondly, be partners, not vendors. If what a client wants is simply someone who will bang out press releases and go through the motions, that client should be working with a freelancer. An agency, on the other hand, should be partners with their clients. They should become truly involved in that client's business and actually help that client drive their business. A pitfall for a lot of younger people in public relations is that they don't take the time to really learn their client's business and industry. That lack of fundamental understanding can be very destructive on any account.

Measuring Return on Investment

Many clients want to know how to measure the value of public relations; basically, they want to know how to determine that they get what they pay for. A variety of tools and methods can measure the effects and goals of public relations. Traditionally, public relations has been measured on the basis of the number of clips received and the circulation figures those clips amount to, compared to advertising equivalency. While this method has been a long-standing system of evaluations, it really doesn't do much for the more sophisticated client looking for something more than just knowing they got space in a paper that reached however many people. Other tools include a greater analysis of the content of the stories that were published or broadcast. You break these stories down by each story's ability to drive your message point, by geography, by the publications or broadcast outlets they appeared in. Were these outlets on your key priority list?

On the other hand there are a lot of other ways to measure success. We like to measure the leads produced as a result of public relations. We do this by setting up a mechanism within the client, so they understand how to ascertain whether a lead produced came from advertising, public relations, direct mail, or word of mouth. It must be tracked so that everyone understands exactly where the lead was generated. Public relations can play an important role in lead generation. We may not be able to make it drink, but we can bring the horse to the water.

Another source of evaluation is simply sales. We very much like to have our programs measured by sales during a particular time period. You can do this by looking at trend analysis, evaluating where sales were, and then looking at the change in sales after the injection of a public relations campaign. You can further measure that geographically, or by specific stories, or in a number of other ways.

There are many ways to evaluate public relations, but they all get back to how effectively the messages were portrayed, and what the actual results of these messages were. Did they generate new business? Did more leads come in? Did the client's business move forward as a result of what you did? Did your programs change audience perceptions of a company, its brand, or its products?

This obviously brings up issues of compensation. How should a public relations firm be compensated? For actual work done? For success of this work? While it would be nice to have a value compensation, so that if we helped drive a business, we would receive some sort of a reward for it, the reality is that virtually always, we work on an hourly basis, and I think that that is most fair. Agencies get into difficulty when they have a large number of clients on a fixed-fee basis, and those fixed fees don't even begin to compensate them for the actual time they spend on the account. On the other hand, simply working on an hourly basis is not fair to an agency either, because an agency has to put together an account team and maintain it. If the client has a heavy workload one month and almost no workload the next, you still have an account team that has to be paid, and that isn't fair either. So a base fee gives you a minimum amount every month, above which you will also bill on an hourly basis. That base fee, of course, includes a set number of hours, but it allows you to be compensated for any hours above that number.

Keeping House, Keeping Clients, Keeping Current

Leadership is different things to different people. It is not just about becoming involved, but perhaps more importantly, when you are involved, it's about having something constructive to put forward. It's about demonstrating leadership and demonstrating suggestions for the betterment of the business or organization. It's about taking a much longer view and of trying to work within the business to see that the business itself is looking far ahead.

Too often, we are all so absorbed with our clients' business that we are not thinking about where *we* should be going. As practitioners, we can do a better job for our clients if we have a firm handle on the management of our own businesses. There is a tendency for account staff to be solely client-oriented, and that's as it should be. They are concerned with getting a job done, and much less concerned about staying within budgets or creating more effective procedures within the agency. But agency management must be concerned with the agency's bottom line and its strategic approach to future business.

One of the things we always talk about is what we call "closing the back door." This means making sure you are always thinking about your current clients and their needs and retaining them, every bit as much as thinking in terms of attracting new business. If you don't close the back door, what you bring in the front means a lot less to your growth

185

and development, and you are doing nothing more than treading water.

However, perhaps the most often repeated advice around our office is that effort doesn't count – results count. As younger people work in the business, they sometimes get overtaken by the idea that a lot of effort somehow means a lot to the client. It really doesn't. Clients aren't impressed by effort. They are impressed only by the results you can give them. They don't care if you spent X number of hours trying to track down some media. They care only that you actually got it. They don't care if you spent many hours planning an event, unless the event is successful. They want only results, as it should be.

One way to keep your edge in the public relations industry is by keeping current with what's going on in your city, your state, the nation, and internationally. It's also extremely important to keep up with what's happening in your client's industry, so you're able to give your client key information about trends in his industry even before he's aware of them. Another way to keep your edge is by staying active in your own industry. I have tried to do this by serving on the executive board for the Counselor's Academy, the section of the Public Relations Society of America that serves the agency side of the business. In that role I discuss and deal with what is happening in the industry, with best practices and so on. Beyond that I am involved in another organization called Public Relations

Organization International, which is a network group. Within this group I work with people literally all over the world who own independent agencies. We talk often about what is happening in the industry, best practices, and ways to drive both our agencies and the industry forward. And as a partnership of agencies, we assist each other as needed and use each other as resources.

Golden Rules of PR

Understand your client's business. Understand your client's industry. The only way for you to be effective in acting on behalf of your client is to really understand what they are all about. You cannot just whip out a press release and believe you have sufficient information there to attract anybody's interest. If you really understand what your client is trying to do, and you understand it within the context of the industry they are in, then you have a much greater chance of working with the media to reach your audience with the right messages. This point is absolutely critical.

Second, understand the media. You must understand just what materials and information they need to write or to broadcast. You must understand how each organization is set up, who controls whom, and who controls what. You must understand who the specific reporters are in the specific organization and whether or not they will cover your topic. If you do not take these steps, you will have very little chance of taking any information at all from your client to the audience through that medium.

Understanding how to work with a client is essential. Understanding how to be a counselor instead of a vendor is learned over time. Younger people, especially, often don't feel comfortable being in a counselor's role. They need to learn this skill. They must learn to be a counselor and not an order taker to be truly successful. Only when you are a counselor can you really help your client beyond the basic fundamentals of writing a release.

Last and most important, never lie to the media. All it can do is come back to hurt you – badly.

Exploding Technology, Changing Perceptions

Based on what has happened in the past, and projecting forward, it is safe to say public relations will continue to grow in the area of technology. There will be more and more technology to power the industry. The tools we rely on will give us a greater ability to fine tune along the way.

When I began in the industry, we were basically confined to the use of typewriters. Fax machines were only just beginning to appear. It was a very different environment. Today, the Internet and the databases available on it are in wide use. The fundamentals, such as fax machines and computers, are commonly on every desk. As we go into the future, we will see greater use of the Internet for more research and for the dissemination of the news. We will see a personalization of our audiences. In the future, we won't have a mass audience. In just the past 20 years, we have seen an explosion of media. We have gone from a relatively small handful of magazines and daily newspapers to magazines that now cover every imaginable topic. In the future we will capture much more of that online. We will dissect our audiences to a much greater degree. We will be able to get down almost to the individual level in the way we drive messages to them, which will be much more personalized. PR will move away from mass market and much closer to the individual, or at least to small-audience categories.

If I could wave a magic wand, I would change the common perception of public relations. Many believe it is somehow a shallow activity involving nothing more than hustling stories to the media. I would change this perception, so people could grasp the greater understanding of its importance and the benefits it brings, not just to companies but to the people who watch TV, listen to the radio, and read newspapers.

I would also want to change the training necessary to enter the public relations field, making the practice more professional at all levels. That might mean creating higher

189

and more mandatory accreditation, but either way, the end result would be a more professional, more qualified work force.

Thomas L. Amberg is president and CEO of Cushman/Amberg Communications, a national public relations agency headquartered in Chicago, with additional offices in St. Louis and Washington, D.C. He was named president of the agency, then known as Aaron D. Cushman and Associates, in 1991, and purchased the agency in 1997. It was renamed at that time to reflect the new ownership.

Mr. Amberg joined the agency in 1983 after 12 years as a reporter and editor for the St. Louis Globe-Democrat, where he won numerous awards for both political and investigative reporting. During his tenure as a political reporter, he covered politics at the local, state, and national levels. He spent three years in Springfield, Illinois, as bureau chief of the newspaper's office, covering Illinois government, and later covered numerous Congressional, gubernatorial, senatorial, and presidential campaigns. He covered the 1980 Reagan campaign from the day Ronald Reagan announced for the presidency through the election, traveling full-time with the candidate.

In his role as president of Cushman/Amberg Communications, Mr. Amberg oversees all strategic communications planning and actively counsels clients in crisis situations. He serves on the executive committee board of the Counselors Academy, and is Regional Vice President for North America of the Public Relations Organisation International.

Mr. Amberg graduated from Colgate University in 1971 with a BA in political science and earned an MBA from the University of Missouri in 1980.

SMALL BUSINESS BANG! DESIGNING AND LAUNCHING A SUCCESSFUL SMALL BUSINESS PR CAMPAIGN

ROBYN M. SACHS
RMR & Associates
President and
Chief Executive Officer

PR 101: A Necessity, Not a Luxury

What kind of honor is it to be recognized as "Small Business' Best-Kept Secret"? No matter how long you've been in business, customers are less likely to buy from you if they have never heard of your name or product. Name recognition and visibility are the keys to growing your business, and public relations is the way to make your company more visible.

Each big business began as a small company with a plan – not just a business plan, but an integrated marketing plan, one that would introduce its products, services, leaders, and mission into the marketplace using a series of tried-and-true vehicles. In 1987, when I purchased and became president of RMR Advertising, a struggling advertising agency, I knew the only way to climb to the top of our industry was to do for our own company what we do for our clients: solidify our internal messaging, create an awareness campaign, share our firm's message and mission to everyone who would listen, and do it as frequently as possible. RMR Advertising is now RMR & Associates, an integrated advertising, marketing, and public relations agency that caters to emerging growth companies. When I first purchased the company we were only a four-person agency. With a structured plan, a consistent communications effort, and a lot of enthusiasm, we have grown by 600 percent and have been recognized as one of the country's fastest-growing firms.

Even if you don't have a communications powerhouse on staff, you can still tackle and master the basics of good public relations, once you have some direction. In this chapter, you'll learn what public relations can do for a business, why public relations is a necessity, not a luxury, for small businesses, and find many of the pieces to assemble a well-rounded, low-cost, high-return public relations program. Use this chapter as a primer to acquaint yourself with the inner-workings of PR, and remember that since public relations and its vehicles are comprehensive and multi-faceted, no one source will be able give you everything you need.

The Definition of Small Business

There's no question that small business is a substantial part of the nation's economy. It may surprise you to know that 90 percent of all U.S. businesses, or roughly 27 million companies, are small businesses. Small businesses employ 43 million employees, 21 percent of whom are sole proprietors. The official definition of a "small business" fluctuates, but some of the details are clear: The companies have fewer than 100 employees and less than $10 million in revenue. Small businesses also account for $1 trillion in payroll and $5 trillion in annual sales receipts. (Source: The Tower Group, July 2001). It's almost ironic to call the market sector "small" business.

Small businesses compete against not only each other, but also against the giants in the marketplace. That's why PR is so essential; small companies need to make themselves seen and heard in the ever increasing confusion of monster corporations.

The Impact of Public Relations

If a tree falls in the middle of the forest in Oregon, and no one is around to hear it, does it make a noise? It does if an article about that tree is published in *The Register-Guard* and *Oregonian Online* the day it falls. Nothing can disseminate a message, tell a story, rally support, instill confidence, and reinforce loyalty like the third-party credibility that comes from a PR campaign.

A most common misconception about PR is that it's just publicity. This is far from the truth. Publicity is merely getting the word out. PR is a multi-faceted approach to changing the way the public thinks about, feels about, and reacts to a certain company, person, service, or product, by a third-party affirmation. This is also the reason public relations is not advertising. Advertising is a controlled message – planned, purchased, and placed by a company to speak directly to the public. The results of PR are often more credible to the public because the message has been created and shared by an unbiased source.

Another misconception is that a public relations program is a luxury, something very expensive, excessive, and difficult to manage. On the contrary, a PR campaign launched within a small business is easily supervised and fun to implement. With the proper planning, the correct tools at your disposal, and a great deal of persistence, any small business can reap the rewards.

If done right, public relations can help your company do many things:

❏ Establish a premium brand and image
❏ Create high-profile awareness of the brand
❏ Establish a consistent image across all marketing vehicles
❏ Generate qualified sales leads and Web site traffic
❏ Increase the ratio of sales to requests for information
❏ Position your company's executives as industry experts

Branding

What exactly is a "brand"? A brand is a cultural, sensory image that surrounds your company or product and creates an indelible symbol in the minds of your customers; it's an assurance of quality and stability, making the selection worry-free for your customers; it's a significant source of competitive advantage and earning potential; and it's a promise of performance. Remember the foundation of every brand is perceived quality.

Branding is easy to understand if you break it down. The word "brand" is derived from "to burn" – picture the branding iron of the American West. The brand elicits emotions in consumers, affecting perceived reputation, quality, and service. It's not solely about the logo, the theme song, or the celebrity endorsement. It's about influencing the human experience through perception. Knowing this, why wouldn't a small business create a brand for itself?

Take, for example, the little round Sunkist orange. For the most part, its brand is the only thing that makes it different from every other orange in the produce aisle. Yet, consumers are happy to pay 15 cents more on every dollar for the Sunkist orange, primarily because consumers perceive it to be fresher, sweeter, and juicier than its competitors. Here, and in many other instances, brand equity is hugely valuable.

So what does this mean for your small business? The earlier you begin building a brand, the easier it will be and the less it will cost. Start now by scrutinizing your current brands (the name of your company and its products or services). Ask your current customers why they purchased from you, and what feelings your company evokes in them. Since it's the emotion that sells, the better you can understand the emotional basis for your customer's relationship with your brand, the better you can use it to strengthen bonds.

Getting Started

Even though it's vital to your business' welfare, don't enter into a public relations campaign too lightly. Since public relations isn't as clearly and quickly measurable as other programs in a company, it's crucial that the marketing communications manager fully understands what PR can and can't do, and be able to communicate this to upper management. A communications department is not an isolated branch of the business; a well-executed campaign includes participation from all sides.

To determine which path your small business should take, start from the finish: Identify your company's goals; isolate those vehicles that work toward those goals; and allocate funds and resources accordingly. Integrating multiple vehicles will make each vehicle work harder and is more cost effective. Integration lowers the true cost of selling overall.

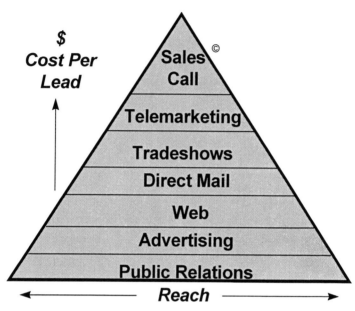

©RMR & Associates, Inc.

As you can see from the tactical implementation triangle, the most expensive way to sell your company is one-on-one sales calls. The most recent estimate is that one sales call costs $500. On the other hand, public relations can reach far more people at a much lower "cost per thousand." A good public relations campaign can result in articles in several different newspapers and publications and reach millions of people. The other benefit of using some of the broader-reaching vehicles, such as public relations and advertising, is that you can get your company name in front of a prospect before the one-on-one sales call and increase the chance of being effective. It is much easier to close a sale if the prospect has already heard of your company. The advantage of using an integrated approach is that you can combine these vehicles based on your needs, your budget, your timeframe, and other variables to get the most effective program for your company.

All CFOs see is the bottom line on the balance sheet; they don't see the stellar relationships with key media, the heightened image and awareness, the increase in market share, and the improved reputation.

Public relations is most important, and therefore, should be better funded, for companies with a high FUD factor. FUD stands for fear, uncertainty, and doubt – an aspect of business that will influence how you approach a communications program. The media, as well as the public, experience FUD when introduced to a new company, product, or service. Technology is one of those industries that benefit from PR over advertising because of the general uncertainty about the products in the market. PR carries more weight in those markets because of its ability to facilitate third-party credibility. Companies with a pricier product also gain more return from public relations because the public is more likely to purchase a big-ticket item from a company that has been validated by the press.

To help the public overcome their FUD, small businesses must use public relations to position themselves as dependable, quality organizations with staying power and growth potential. Outreach must be consistent; messages must be controlled; and news must include growth-oriented information. Once the public is assured that your company is not a fly-by-night business, they'll feel comfortable buying from you.

It's always wise to assess your company's budgetary guidelines and constraints before making any program commitments. Even if you choose to perform most of the public relations functions in-house, you should allocate a budget for collateral and other materials, phone, fax, postage, and travel. Most companies, regardless of size, spend between 1 percent and 20 percent of total revenue on their communications program, depending on their offerings. Small businesses often spend between 5 percent and 10 percent of their total revenue on public relations. Many smaller companies decide to keep their functions in-house to reduce costs, only to realize they're spending more on those resources than agencies already have at their disposal. Agencies can work more efficiently by leveraging the existing relationships they have with the editorial community.

Goal Setting

Setting goals is a task many small businesses do annually. However, setting corporate goals doesn't always take into account integrating corporate messaging with the company's communications plan. First determine the company's goals for the upcoming year:

❏ Initially introduce your company or a new product into the market?
❏ Increase sales or market share?
❏ Increase name, product, service recognition?
❏ Improve your company's (its executives') reputation?

Once the company's goals are established, the PR team needs to align their efforts with the company's current focus. Public relations campaigns, while ongoing and consistent, do take on short-term, project-style features when news is in the pipeline. In the goal-setting stage, it is important to lay out your expected results for the marketing team, so they can strive to meet your goals. You will revisit these initial projections at the end of the campaign to measure how well your goals were reached through public relations efforts.

To attain measurable results, it is best to write out your goals at the beginning of the campaign. Having something concrete by which to measure your achievements will enable you to judge the effectiveness or success of the public relations program. This goal-setting stage should include evaluating the number of briefings you expect to be set, selecting the top five publications in which you want to get placements, and determining whether getting a cover story is a must-have. If you are introducing a new product, you should establish the number of product reviews you expect to see. If you are trying to raise awareness of your company and increase your name recognition, determine how you expect to measure those somewhat intangible results. Do you expect to have editors refer to you in articles, and conference coordinators to call you to speak at local or industry events? These goals should be realistic. Don't go into a project demanding a cover story in an industry-renowned publication, only to realize after the campaign is completed that the news wasn't that exciting. Once you determine your goals, you can choose those vehicles that will help fulfill them.

Research, Planning, and Preparation

You must complete numerous activities before embarking on a public relations campaign, including market research and competitive analysis. Before choosing your public relations vehicles, you should determine whether your goal is to better position yourself against other products, other markets, or other companies. If you want to conduct a full-blown market research program, I recommend you hire a marketing firm to conduct these activities for you before your PR campaign, since they can be very complex and time-consuming.

The second step is identifying your company spokesperson(s). Ideally, your spokesperson should be the highest-ranking executive possible, and he or she should have the expertise to handle the toughest questions. Your spokesperson should be the "voice of the company" in articles, on talk shows, and at conferences; however, when members of the media call the company directly (and this will happen more and more as you become a reliable resource for editors), the calls should be directed to the marketing communications manager, not the spokesperson, so the manager can prepare the spokesperson for responding to the nature of the call.

Next, develop a list of key media outlets. This "core list" of media targets is the skeleton of your media relations program. Savvy practitioners realize that 20 percent of the individuals in a market will influence the other 80 percent. You should identify groups of influential publications, including local and national print, broadcast, and online media outlets in those markets and trade categories that reach and influence your publics. And don't forget industry analysts, as well. Your extended list should include name, title, e-mail and mailing addresses (mailing address and street address may be different), and phone and fax numbers. Other essential information should include preferred method of material receipt and deadlines (both day and time).

Each of the media outlets has a schedule of topics they plan to write on in upcoming issues, called an editorial calendar. Authored article opportunities, speaking opportunities, and award nominations are also on a schedule and have their own calendars. If you have time, select those articles within all the target outlets that your spokesperson is qualified to comment on, as well as all the authored article and award opportunities you'd like to apply for, and create your own opportunities spreadsheet. Cultivating long-term relationships with these editors can lead to articles that educate your target market, while at the same time educating the publications' readers.

Once you've determined your target audience and your spokesperson, you need to identify who in your organization will be conducting your outreach. This is where a public relations or media relations agency is beneficial, but if you have staff members who meet the following criteria, they'll do just fine.

❑ Who in your company are your biggest cheerleaders?
❑ Who has the best attitude?
❑ Who are the most dedicated and persistent in their positions?
❑ And most importantly, who can look rejection in the eye, time after time, day after day, and still come out fighting for your company's cause?

If you're lucky enough to have one or two of these dynamos in your organization, congratulations! You have now pinpointed your media relations team, and you're ready to prepare your arsenal of media relations supplies.

Media kits help you get most of your relevant information out in one neat package, and, in turn, help editors do their jobs more effectively. Anything that makes an editor's job easier increases your opportunities for exposure. Build your kit to ensure it's a functional and accurate presentation of your company's product and services. A media kit serves as an introductory piece to editors, analysts, investors, and partners. A comprehensive kit includes the following:

❑ Recent press releases
❑ Company background information
❑ Biographies of spokespeople (You may want to include a headshot if the spokesperson is speaking at a tradeshow where the kit is being distributed.)
❑ Case histories, testimonials, customer quotes
❑ Article reprints
❑ Product or service materials
❑ FAQ or fact sheet
❑ Customer or reference list
❑ PowerPoint presentation snippets (once again, if a representative from the company is speaking at a tradeshow where the kit is being distributed)
❑ Business card of the primary communications contact at your company (This is very important for a number of reasons, not the least of which is media accessibility.)

As a rule, the contents of a media kit are more important than the format you present them in, but you want to ensure that the whole package accurately represents the culture of your company. A high-end, full-color, glossy folder will make your business look successful and well established, but you don't want to blow your entire budget on printing (and reporters know you're bluffing if your kit is snazzier than Microsoft's). On the other hand, if you package your materials in a taped-up manila folder, you also send the wrong signal. Despite the emphasis on a "paperless environment," many editors still prefer a hard-copy media kit to electronic documents.

You should have enough media kits to send to each of your most important editorial contacts, and even more if you plan to exhibit or speak at conferences or tradeshows. It is a good rule of thumb to also reproduce the media kit components on your Web site.

Ready for Take-Off: PR Vehicles

On any journey, choosing the right vehicle determines when, and if, you'll reach your destination. The public relations journey is no different. For each type of journey, an array of vehicles is ready to deliver you there. Planning is key. Different combinations of vehicles can accomplish different things. Depending on your goals and your budget, you may want to use some vehicles more often, some less often, and some not at all. Review the descriptions, uses, and outcomes of the vehicles below to see which ones are best suited for your business.

Press Releases

Press releases are the most efficient way to communicate your news to the press, and a great way to disseminate your message exactly the way you want. A word of caution: Make sure your news is worthy before launching into the release writing and distribution process. Fluffy news only wastes your time, as well as that of the reporters you're sending it to, making your company look less credible in the eyes of the publication. Remember the editor's WIIFM rule: What's In It For Me? If an editor looks at the headline of your press release and asks himself, "Why should I care?" it's not a newsworthy topic. Keep in mind that you should know your audience before you distribute your news to them. Not every publication and writer should get every one of your press releases. Determine who should be on your distribution list based on the type of news you are announcing. Product review editors should get new product announcements. New hires or new office space announcements should go only to editors at your local paper.

It also helps to write your releases in the style editors are used to – the inverted pyramid. Put the most important information in the first paragraph, and use the following paragraphs to fill in the details. If a reporter is getting 200 press releases every day, you want to make sure yours cuts through the clutter and captures him in the first paragraph. The golden rule of press releases is the shorter the better.

You want to make sure that if the reporter has time to read only your first paragraph, he'll get your news.

There are many ways to distribute press releases. If you do it in-house (the most cost-effective, yet time-consuming method), make sure you send them the way your editors and analysts most prefer – mail, fax, e-mail, or courier. If you decide to use a newswire distribution service, research your options, and find the service that best reaches your intended markets for the lowest price. You may have to supplement your distribution through in-house methods anyway, depending on your market. Hint: Send your releases to your current and prospective customers, too!

Media Relations

This vehicle is not an option – it's a requirement! Media relations is proactive, consistent contact with editors in your market space. This is sometimes considered the most difficult public relations vehicle to integrate into a small business' communications plan, as it requires steadfast contact with the media. Media relations is a process that works only when it's constant and carefully crafted. This makes it challenging if a small business tries to keep their marketing efforts in-house because media relations demands the attention of one or two dedicated marketing professionals who have the time and energy to constantly funnel news to the press and keep them up-to-date on the company's latest announcements. However, media relations is also the most rewarding public relations vehicle, as it often leads to your best placements. Developing strong relationships with the reporters and editors who focus on your industry will result in quality articles.

Media relations is by far most difficult in the beginning of the program. Reporters experience fear, uncertainty, and doubt (FUD) when dealing with smaller, lesser-known companies with new, unproven products and services. Because of this uncertainty, it's harder to cut through the clutter, so it's important to be honest, helpful, and patient with the media. There is one advantage to reporters when dealing with small businesses: easier, quicker access to high-level executives.

The Internet has changed the dynamics of media relations. E-mail gets you right into a reporter's office, straight to the desktop, but your message can be deleted as quickly as it was opened. Don't spam, and don't send unsolicited e-mails. E-mail can cut press release distribution costs and reach those media outlets that wire services miss, but you should let reporters know why you're contacting them, and offer them an out if they're not interested in receiving more information from you. Courtesy goes a long way with reporters; don't take easy access for granted.

Although you want to contact reporters while they're working on an article relevant to your business, missed opportunities can still become future opportunities. For example, if you see an article that's written about one of your competitors or a trend story you think you should have been included in, you can use this moment to turn your company into a source. Call the reporter to tell him you saw his article, and because your company is very heavily involved in that market you'd like to tell him a little bit about what you're doing. After all, the reporter's primary function, like yours, is to inform the marketplace. A similar concept is latching on to a current event. For example, if your company manufactures security equipment, and the latest news in your community is focused on high school robberies, you can call your local print and broadcast media and offer your spokesperson's expertise for inclusion in a related piece.

Media relations also complements other vehicles. For instance, when you drop a press release, you should always follow up with a phone call or e-mail to explain to the reporter why this news should matter to him or her. As I mentioned before, reporters and editors get deluged with releases. You need to help them focus on your news.

(Note: Some smaller companies I've worked with have tried hiring a full-time person to be the media relations component, but found them being pulled into other aspects of the marketing effort, losing sight of the media relations goals. This is one vehicle that is best fulfilled by a team of media relations specialists at an agency. You'll be so thankful you outsourced this function.)

Media Training

Now that you've chosen your spokesperson, you must get started on media training right away. This should include identifying and memorizing the company's key message points, preparing the speaker for awkward questions, and teaching repetition and bridging techniques to ensure your spokesperson stays focused on the key message points. Ideally, your messages will be included, verbatim, in the interviewer's article. Many PR firms have media training capabilities that include video- and audio-taping to prepare for broadcast interviews. One thing to remember about media training is that you want to limit yourself to between three and five message points, and be sure to stick with them. Editors won't remember more than that. To be most effective, the message points should be phrased as benefits or differentiators and repeated as often as possible.

Briefings

Face-to-face briefings are a great way to build company recognition and trust with the media. Your spokesperson can tell reporters "the story behind the story," demonstrate the product or service your company provides, and comment on current topics within your industry. Use your

:etings to develop long-term relationships with editors, ther than a one-time pitch and run.

Briefings can be scheduled while your media relations team is making calls on behalf of your latest news. Editors are seldom able to leave the newsroom, so offer to stop by their offices at lunch, or just after deadlines close, with food. Since time is limited, don't waste it. Take a media kit, your strongest messages, and solid insight into the writer's beat for best results.

Speaking Engagements

Arranging for experts in your company to speak at industry conferences, tradeshows, association meetings, seminars, or other forums allows direct contact with those decision-makers within your peer, customer, and vertical market groups. But remember these are not self-promotional excursions. You really want to make sure you're speaking to the audience and giving them information they can use, not merely plugging your product or service. Address the needs of the audience with relevant information.

Tradeshows

If you've decided to make a large financial and time commitment by exhibiting at a tradeshow, break through the clutter of all those competitors by pre-briefing attending editors with your announcements before the show. This not only gets you more attention; it actually causes editors to specifically search for your booth. Save some information for the show itself, however, so you have a reason to meet with the press again. You should also leave your briefing materials in pressrooms and information kiosks and post them online through the organizer of the show.

Case Histories

Effective case histories are stories written in a "problem, solution, results" format, showing your target audience how customers benefited from using your product or service. By showing how your company solved a real-life customer problem, you not only add credibility to your message, but you also help editors flesh out stories by providing them additional sources. Make sure you get approval before you use one of your customers as a reference. Also, try to get them on board with the message points you most want to stress. It's great publicity for their company too, so it's a two-way street. You can get a lot of mileage from case histories: Your sales people can take them on calls or pitches, and you can include them in your advertising campaign.

Awards

Corporate and product awards add credibility to your organization and message, but they rarely "just happen" on their own. Learn about the nomination process by speaking with the review boards, past winners, and judges. The time spent researching and applying for awards can be the most productive time you ever spend because you uncover more in-depth information about your business. Your clients and customers will also like buying from a "winner."

Authored Articles

These bylined articles help position you and your company as authorities in your market space. They don't necessarily have to be written by the individuals at your organization. Good PR agencies work with freelancers who ghost-write articles on behalf of their clients. So if an opportunity arises where an editor is looking for an authored article, your expert doesn't have to take the time to write it on his or her own. And once the article is written, you can use it as a sales tool by sending reprints to your current and potential customers. Frequently, the articles can be leveraged as speaking topics, as well.

Community Relations

If your company's budget and resources can support it, community relations is a fun and effective way to connect with your customers, while strengthening the image and reputation of the business. By spearheading or sponsoring community events, your company can demonstrate its commitment to providing for the neighborhood and the people in it. If your small business is consumer-focused, hand out samples of your product at the event. If your company attracts business customers, donate your product or service to a school, community center, or non-profit organization. These feel-good sponsorships are great fodder for other PR vehicles: press releases, case histories, and campaign award nominations.

Web Site

Even if you don't plan to sell anything online, you cannot afford to disregard the power of the Internet. Gone are the days when your customers pull out the Yellow Pages or dial directory assistance. With the Internet, you can welcome your customers and potential customers into your world with just a few clicks. Make sure your site has the same look and feel, and similar content, as your other marketing materials, and that it's easy to navigate. Some important links or pages your site should contain include:

❑ Company background
❑ Description of products and services
❑ Contacts (who's who and what they do)
❑ Media room
❑ Testimonials
❑ FAQs

All PR vehicles serve a purpose, but some vehicles are more important to small businesses than others. My experience tells me that the three most essential PR vehicles are media relations, speaking engagements, and authored articles. These three allow you to advance your position in your industry, help you reach your target audiences, and attract customers more efficiently.

Small businesses have an advantage over large corporations when it comes to making the most of current events and trends. There are fewer approvals to get when the marketing department wants to launch a new campaign. Smaller companies have a better focus on their market segment. Because small businesses have that one-to-one interaction with a customer base, they understand problems and pains better.

Public relations success is spelled with three P's: persistence, perseverance, and propensity for action. No PR plan, no matter how well-thought or well-funded, will work if the people executing the program aren't in it 100 percent. Relations with the media take time to cultivate and may not always bring the desired results, but it's crucial to continue.

Weekly meetings are also vital to your program. Rally the troops over bagels and coffee, and invite them to share ideas, challenges, and successes from the previous week. These meetings also give you a chance to communicate goings-on in other departments, especially those that have an impact on marketing activities (new product developments, new hires, changes in service offerings).

Corporate Identity – Look and Feel of Your Business

A corporate identity package will give your small business a big-business image and is significant in the branding process. You can get a lot of mileage from a well-designed identity package that accurately represents your company's offerings. Any good marketing or advertising agency can create a logo and help you choose colors that you'll carry through your entire communications campaign, from business cards and letterhead to direct mail to your ad campaign (dream big!). Even if your budget isn't as big as your dreams, you'll be able to develop some of these pieces for relatively low cost:

❑ Corporate logo
❑ Corporate brochure
❑ Letterhead and envelopes
❑ Mailing labels
❑ Business cards

Results

Just as you begin with research, you should end with research. No public relations campaign is over until you figure out whether, and how, you've met your goals. Why is the "how" important? Because if the vehicles you've chosen aren't working, you should try something else.

The first "how" is to conduct another round of market research to determine whether your target audience was affected by your communications and outreach efforts. Are consumers more aware of your company name and product? Has there been an increase in demand for your product or service? Is your Web site getting more traffic and inquiries? The marketing agency you used before launching the PR campaign can help you with the follow-up market research.

Tracking results can include tangible figures, such as the number of placements, hits, and speaking engagements, and hard numbers, such as advertising equivalencies – a dollar figure that identifies what the placement would have been worth if you had had to buy the equivalent ad space. Measurable results can also include intangibles, such as evaluating an article to determine the tone (positive or negative) and whether your key message points were cited. An article that highlights your company and product in a positive light should be worth much more than one that inaccurately portrays who you are and what you do.

With the help of a media clipping service, you can evaluate media relations in-house. For a monthly fee and per-clip charge, media clipping services scan print, broadcast, and online media outlets for mentions of your company, and provide them to you. This is the best way to track where you're getting coverage, and it's nearly impossible to do it on your own – you'd have to subscribe to and read every publication you sent your releases to.

To evaluate your media efforts, choose your qualifiers based on your goals, for instance, "relevant media outlet?", "accurate message?" or "proximate to press release drop?" What good is an article in *Road & Track* if your product is a sofa bed? Once your qualifiers are in place, use them to rate each placement. When you're finished, find your success percentage by dividing the number of on-target placements with the number of overall placements. Now that's measuring public relations success one article at a time.

Beyond the Campaign: Consistency is Key

Once you've established and initiated your public relations program, you need to remember that everything your company does, and every word your employees speak on behalf of the company, is a reflection of the business. Make sure your automated voicemail system works well, is easy to navigate, and reflects your company's culture. If you have a receptionist, that person should be trained in customer service, as he or she is the first impression your customers and prospects encounter. Suggest to your staff that they don't discuss internal business in public (especially problems) and that they wear their logo attire to events, and with pride. Encourage them not to speak to the media directly, but to point the media in the direction of the spokesperson, who has completed media training. Remember that perception is reality, and your employees are ambassadors of your business. And while the media contact should be limited to the spokesperson, be sure the entire company knows the messaging and branding and has a comprehensive understanding of where the company is going.

The Challenges

Time is certainly a challenge every business faces, and small businesses feel the crunch even more profoundly. It's easy to lose focus and momentum when other tasks are looming over you and your department, but remember that PR is an ongoing activity, and to abandon it only hurts your company. If you decide to keep your public relations in-house, you must be able to dedicate one or two full-time staff members to promoting your company. A safe schedule for public relations activity is one day a week (or four days out of the month). This doesn't have to mean you should be calling editors once a week to harass them with each little news tidbit. But it does mean you designate someone in your company to review your company's marketing communications efforts to make sure a consistent message is being delivered to the media, so your company remains visible. This allows you to be constant with your outreach, yet doesn't overtake your other responsibilities (or those of your staff).

Budget is also always a challenge, but if you determine your budget early in the program and set realistic expectations, you can construct a public relations campaign that has the same impact as those on a larger scale.

No Magic, No Secret Code

If all this direction is getting you lost, you may want to work with an agency. Don't feel intimidated by the thought of hiring an agency to implement your PR campaign; agencies and their well-trained professionals act as an extension to your in-house team and can save you time and frustration.

One of the best ways to choose an agency is through a referral. Talk to other small business owners in your area to see who they've used or heard of. If that isn't helpful, contact the Council of Public Relations Firms at www.prfirms.org. Through its site, you can select a PR firm based on location, size, disciplines, and other factors. Many of the firms listed there have been audited by the Council and have very good reputations. When reviewing agencies, remember to ask about other clients (Will your small company get lost in the crowd of larger clients?), team composition (Who exactly will you be working with?), and billing methods (project versus retainer billing).

Remember that someone in your company must be the main contact for your agency. Although your agency team will help you identify and implement your goals, messages, and vehicles, don't rely on them to run the campaign for you. Weekly meetings are a must, and in them, be prepared to talk about progress, challenges, and new ideas (much as you would if you constructed a team in-house). Nothing enhances a client-agency relationship like outstanding communication.

Public relations has no secret code and no strange ingredients, but it can do magic for your small business. It's also an excellent way to bring your company's departments together, stay connected with your customers, and make a name for yourself in your community and industry. With some planning, persistence, and a little luck, your business can reap the reward of public relations.

Robyn M. Sachs has served as president and CEO of RMR & Associates since purchasing the company in 1987. Over the years, RMR has earned recognition for aggressive campaigns that produce measurable results. In 2000, RMR was named the 10th fastest-growing agency in the United States and the fastest-growing agency in Maryland by PRWEEK. RMR has also been awarded a "MC Icon

Award" for best branding campaign in the country for their work with PSINet and an "ADDY Award" for the best commercial Web site by the Ad Club of Washington, D.C., in 1997.

In 1998, Ernst & Young awarded the "Entrepreneur of the Year Award" to Ms. Sachs and the agency. Additionally, the Washington Business Journal has recognized the agency as one of the Top 25 Advertising Agencies and Top 25 Public Relations Firms annually since 1991 and included RMR in its listing of Washington's largest women-owned businesses since 1990.

PR: A KEY DRIVER OF BRAND MARKETING

PATRICE A. TANAKA
Patrice Tanaka & Company, Inc.
Chief Executive Officer and
Creative Director

Thrills, Chills, and a Bit o' the Bubbly

Our specialty is brand-building, consumer-marketing public relations. When a prospective client comes to us, it is usually an assignment to help them increase brand awareness and trial of their product or service. Our ultimate goal is to help clients move the needle on sales.

The most challenging aspect of PR is that the means of success is not totally within our control. We always look at advertising as those "oh-so-lucky-guys" who can actually create a message and buy space or time in the appropriate media to run this message. That's a lot of control that we do not have in public relations, and it can be frustrating, especially when we are trying to provide strong support for a client. Say, for example, our client is launching a new product; ideally, the PR campaign should be timed precisely for when the product is hitting the shelves. Many times we are successful in this regard; sometimes we are not because, again, we do not have total control over when the media coverage is going to appear. What effective PR does accomplish is to help generate valuable, third-party endorsements of a client's product or service. This is often much more credible and powerful than client-sponsored advertising. Effective PR can also help educate customers about a brand in a more in-depth way than is possible with, for example, advertising.

The most exciting aspect of public relations is delivering meaningful results to clients. An example is our ten-year-old cause-related marketing program for client Liz Claiborne, involving the issue of domestic violence. The result has been a very powerful, award-winning campaign that has helped reposition domestic violence from a private, hidden, family matter to a public health crisis, which is key to mobilizing the resources necessary to help end abuse. Liz Claiborne's pioneering work has been good for the domestic violence issue and good for reinforcing the company's position as one that cares about women.

It's thrilling for us to create successful brand-building PR programs that exist only because we thought them up. An example of this is Korbel Champagne's Department of Romance, Weddings & Entertaining – a first-of-its-kind corporate department that associated the brand with all of the occasions when people celebrate with the bubbly. This four-year campaign generated two billion consumer impressions for Korbel, which helped drive the brand's growth from 800,000 to 1.2 million case sales in a declining champagne/sparkling wine category. We can cite equally dramatic case studies for brands such as All-Clad Metalcrafters, Avon Products, Godiva Chocolatier, Microsoft, and Wyndham Hotels & Resorts, among other clients. At our firm, we love the opportunity to create breakthrough PR programs that really make a difference to our clients in growing their brands.

Creating Breakthrough Campaigns

The key measurement of success for our firm is the quality and longevity of our relationships with clients, employees, the media, and our valued business partners. Specifically, in terms of creating a successful long-term client relationship, it is about continuing to deliver meaningful business results that help these organizations achieve their marketing and corporate objectives.

If a marketer wants to bring their brand to life and have it communicate and interact with its target customers, they need to support it with a robust public relations campaign. The role of public relations is to communicate the relevance of the brand to its target customers and, when necessary, help to evolve the brand's positioning, so it continues to remain relevant to this audience. A brand that wants to remain relevant has to evolve correspondingly with its target audience's changing needs, desires, concerns, and issues. This might involve changing brand strategies, or maybe just developing and implementing new tactics to freshen the brand-marketing PR program. It might not be a change in strategy, so much as a change in tactics.

A campaign to build a brand starts with identifying the essence of a client's brand that distinguishes it from the competition. We always hope there is something truly distinctive about the brand that can't be said by the competition or can't be said as convincingly or as credibly by the competition. Our job is to communicate that brand-essence, or soul of the brand, in a very compelling and memorable way to its target audience. A public relations campaign can bring a brand to life only if it is relevant in some way to its target audience: There has to be some reason they should care. If you have crafted your PR messages and campaign in such a way that they address the things that are topmost on customers' minds and the issues they grapple with on an ongoing basis, you have a good chance of making your brand come to life because it addresses a real need. Every campaign has different goals, depending on what the client is seeking to achieve.

Who are our best clients? Our best clients embrace us fully as partners, share their proprietary information and research with us, and help us to understand their needs, desires, objectives, challenges, and obstacles to success. An ideal client brings us into their confidence, so we can be fully informed when we are trying to come up with a breakthrough PR program that is specifically designed to address their brand marketing and corporate objectives. An ideal client trusts that we will do our best work for them and holds us accountable for doing so. Trust and honoring your commitments are at the heart of great client/agency relationships.

In fact, that brings me to the "golden rule" of PR, which is the same as in life: Treat others as you would have them treat you. That rule applies across all business, not just PR.

231

For me, building a strong, enduring business or brand involves honoring your commitments, every day, to all of your constituencies. For our agency that includes employees, clients, media, vendors, the PR community, and the public at large. Honoring our commitments to all of these different stakeholder audiences is the way enduring brands, including PR agency brands, are built.

The process of developing a brand PR program involves immersing ourselves in every available piece of secondary research. If we have the luxury of time and budget, we like to conduct our own primary research, just to test some of our own hypotheses in terms of consumer awareness, perception, attitudes, and behaviors toward the client's brand or category. We try to glean intelligence from industry analysts and consultants and trade and consumer media that cover that industry and, importantly, from customers of the brand. We immerse ourselves in everything we can learn about the client, their competition, and their category. We then use this knowledge base to understand and assess a client's objectives and their brand positioning goals.

Also key to developing the PR campaign is knowing the client's budget and time-frame. Sometimes it's, "We need to launch this new product or service a year from now," and sometimes, "The competition is moving up their launch date, so we're moving ours up to next month – six months earlier than scheduled." The lead time and the budget will determine, in large part, our PR program recommendation to the client.

At our firm, we're big believers in PR as one of the elements in a comprehensive marketing program. We want advertising, direct marketing, interactive, sales promotion, POP – every discipline, including public relations, all to work together to support the brand marketing strategy. If all elements of the marketing mix work together in a synergistic fashion, it is the most efficient and effective type of brand marketing.

Public relations strategies can vary widely, depending on the available budget. When the budget is tight, solid media relations is probably the most cost-effective approach: Target the appropriate media, whether trade or consumer, and communicate your client's story in a compelling way. Present a case for why journalists should do the story you are seeking. There are other low-cost, very efficient ways to generate publicity, such as conducting fairly inexpensive omnibus research, which can be used as a news hook for media coverage. Probably my favorite low-cost PR tactic is one we employed for Korbel Champagne when we created their Department of "Romance, Weddings & Entertaining." We decided to launch our search for the Director of Romance in a manner that was in and of itself a news-generating opportunity. We created and ran an ad in the classifieds section of *The Wall Street Journal* for a Director of Romance. The ad was about four by five inches and cost us only $6,000, but it generated millions of dollars' worth of media coverage. Moreover, we received more than 1,000 resumes from *The Wall Street Journal* readers, including bankers, lawyers, and celebrities, who were all hungry for a little romance in their lives. And, ultimately, we did hire our Director of Romance from one of the many respondents to the ad. The ROI on this $6,000 ad was tremendous.

When the PR budget is generous, we have a lengthy Christmas wish list of PR tactics, including everything from producing a documentary, to staging a major launch event, orchestrating a world tour, hiring a celebrity spokesperson or spokespersons, and conducting a 25- to 30-market program of radio promotions and retailer tie-ins. We also like national consumer sweepstakes where the prize is over-the-top, for example, something like "Win your own private tropical island," or "Take a year-long sabbatical from your job." We love employing advertising to communicate the messages of our PR campaigns. Other big-ticket PR initiatives we like involve conducting a major longitudinal research study, not like the quick-and-dirty omnibus studies, but a major piece of research that could represent huge opportunities for generating brand media coverage.

Measuring return on investment is an ongoing subject of debate and discussion in the PR industry and, unfortunately, no one has come up with the gold standard. So every agency and client measures results in a different way. I think the ultimate measurement of results for an agency like ours, specializing in marketing PR, is increased awareness and trial of our client's brand. And the bottom line: Have we moved the needle on sales for them? Sometimes it is hard to know exactly what the results are and how trackable they are, specifically to the PR component of the marketing campaign. Many times we must base our measurement of how effective our PR program is in terms of tangible things that we produce for clients, such as the quality and quantity of media results. It is, at best, a very crude way of measuring PR results.

To be innovative in public relations, you need to have an orientation toward doing breakthrough work. By this we mean a PR campaign that is strategic, involves some element of a breakthrough creative idea, and succeeds in communicating key client messages. At our firm we approach every assignment as an opportunity to do case-study work. Because this is our going-in position on every assignment, we end up creating a lot of breakthrough PR campaigns.

Pitfalls and Great Advice

One of the major pitfalls in public relations is not anticipating the worst-case scenario for clients, so we and they can be prepared, should the worst case occur. As PR professionals, we must be prepared to deal with client crises because every client will experience one at some time or another. Another common pitfall is accepting at face value our clients' "truths" about their brands or their companies, or even their forecasts for what to expect to happen in their industry. As savvy PR counselors, we need to do our own research and thinking and have our own sense of where our client's brand and their category are going, independent of what they might tell us, so we can counsel them from an informed perspective. Another pitfall to avoid is doing what the client wants when you know it is not in their best interest or the best interest of the brand.

Probably the most important piece of advice I've ever received in terms of building our PR agency was to diversify our client base. We now work in about 15 to 18 different consumer categories. That's very exciting because every new category is a learning experience. When we're working in a new category, we can't just get by on our industry knowledge; we have to learn everything like a complete novice without the benefit of having formed judgments based on prevailing wisdom. We've done some of our best work in these situations because we approach the subject from a fresh, new perspective.

Diversifying your client base does two things. First, it makes your business less vulnerable than if you specialized in any one industry. Second, it helps you maintain your edge by constantly forcing you to learn and become an expert on new subject areas.

To be a leader in PR takes someone who is passionate and committed to doing great work. You must set the example, and however you behave and whatever you espouse are what other people will see, hear, and take their lead from. This is true of leaders in all fields. A strong leader, like a strong company or brand, has to stand for something. If they remain true to their core values through good times and bad times, they will build a strong brand for themselves that is distinctive and that sets them apart from their competition.

Endless Curiosity

To succeed in public relations, you have to have a lot of passion for the work you do and, importantly, you must have incredible perseverance because PR can be a very frustrating profession. As I mentioned earlier, we often do not have complete control over the means to our success. Being an optimist is important, because only if you truly believe things will work out will you be able to consistently manifest that as an outcome. You should also have a keen interest in problem-solving. If you dislike problem-solving and find it difficult to think on your feet, PR is definitely not the career for you. Successful PR people also have an endless curiosity about the world, how things work, and the interrelatedness of people, places and things. They are committed to continuous learning; they have excellent people skills; they are students of human behavior; they are intensely active listeners; and they have strong communication skills. They are also flexible – flexibility is key to success in business and in life. A good PR person should also have a sense of humor and an ability to put things into perspective. The best PR people also exhibit grace under pressure. Because this is a high-stress profession, the degree to which you can remain calm and centered, focused and alert, determines your ability to counsel clients and help them think through their problems.

It is really important as a PR professional to push yourself to continuously learn about things you know little or nothing about. There is a lot going on in the world, new developments are happening all of the time. Sometimes you can slip into a comfort zone of knowing only what you need to know to do your job and if you fall into that mode it can be very dangerous. I am a baby boomer in my 40s, and it takes real work for me to stay abreast of what the 20-somethings in our office think is cool and important. But, in this line of work, it is imperative that I do.

It's really important, as I mentioned previously, to be passionate about your work. If your job does not excite you, then you should find one that does. At our firm, we take on only clients we feel passionate about – because we either love the brand or love the category. There has to be some strong interest or desire on our part for us to take on an assignment. That's our strongest guarantee of doing great work. If it is a client or an industry that we are not really interested in, we will walk away from the assignment, rather than risk doing mediocre work because we're not excited, inspired, and fully engaged. Our goal is to create great work, a great workplace, and great communities that work. We cannot do any of this if we're not personally engaged and excited about the work we do and the people with whom we work.

Creating Communities of Support

Communications technology has dramatically changed the practice of public relations. To be able to communicate and interact one-to-one with individuals in a target population for a client is really amazing. The more we can develop this capability, the more we will be able to tailor the communications and offerings to individuals in a target population. It won't just be a blast e-mail – the same e-mail, the same offer – to everybody who has ever purchased Godiva. It will be customized messages and offers to every Godiva customer.

My greatest wish in terms of changes in public relations is for the profession to have a better reputation than it does. There are many talented PR professionals who work very hard and who always try to do their best for clients. But PR people suffer from a reputation for being unprofessional, untrustworthy, and unethical. The solution may be to have some kind of mandatory training and certification for PR practitioners. Right now we do have an APR accreditation that the Public Relations Society of America offers, but it is strictly voluntary.

Public relations agencies should also avoid taking on questionable clients, as this may create divisiveness within the agency and crises of conscience for their employees. I feel strongly also that public relations agencies should not do spec PR programs for prospective clients because, essentially, we are just giving away our work, our intellectual property, and devaluing it in the process for the sake of winning a piece of business. PR agencies should also be paid royalties for their intellectual property – not just for the time we put into developing and implementing client programs. We should receive royalties on programs we create for clients that they trademark. Another way to improve the image of public relations might be for the industry to do a major national pro bono public service campaign – a la what the advertising industry does through the Advertising Council. Some or all of these initiatives might help us to enhance the image of the PR profession.

In the future, I think brand-marketing PR professionals will be engaged in helping clients create communities of support for their brands via more direct, one-on-one communication with all of their many stakeholder audiences. This will enable brands and organizations to interact more effectively with their customers and, in doing so, deepen and enhance these relationships and, ultimately, build strong, supportive communities that will sustain them through good and bad times in the economy.

Patrice A. Tanaka ("PT") co-founded PT&Co. in July 1990 upon completing a successful management buyback of her public relations firm from former parent company, Chiat/Day, inc. advertising. She is chief executive officer and creative director of PT&Co.

Over the past 11 years, Ms. Tanaka has led PT&Co. to become one of the nation's most highly regarded independent PR firms. During that time, the agency has grown more than 850 percent, won 150+ industry awards for its breakthrough PR campaigns, been celebrated by Inside PR magazine as the "#1 Hot Creative Shop" in the country, and been saluted by Working Mother as one of "15 family-friendly workplaces in America."

Ms. Tanaka has been honored by a number of organizations, including Asian Women in Business (AWIB), which saluted her with its "Entrepreneurial Leadership Award" (October 2001); The Star Group, which honored her as one of the "Leading Women Entrepreneurs of the World" (May 2001); Inside PR magazine, which recognized her as a "Creativity All-Star" (2000); Asian Enterprise magazine, which named her "Asian Entrepreneur of the Year" (1999); Business & Professional Women/U.S.A. which bestowed upon her its "Women Mean

Business Award"(1999); New York Women in Communications, which presented her with the "Matrix" Award (1997) in Public Relations; the Girl Scout Council of Greater New York, which honored her with a "Women of Distinction" Award (1995); the YWCA, which named her to its "Academy of Women Achievers" (1994); and Working Mother magazine with its "Mothering That Works" Award (1994) for creating a family-friendly workplace.

Ms. Tanaka currently serves on the boards of the Asian Pacific American Women's Leadership Institute, the Family Violence Prevention Fund, the Girl Scout Council of Greater New York, New York Women in Communications, where she is now president-elect, and the U.S. Fund for UNICEF. Ms. Tanaka is also a founding board member of the PR agency trade association, the Council of PR Firms.

Ms. Tanaka was born and raised in Hawaii and is a graduate of the University of Hawaii (1974).

AN ESSENTIAL FUNCTION IN A DEMOCRATIC SOCIETY

DAVID FINN
Ruder Finn Group
Chairman

PR From Every Angle

Since I have spent a lifetime as a public relations practitioner and another lifetime as a photographer of sculpture, I have long believed there is something similar about these two kinds of activities. When photographing a work of sculpture, you have to learn to look at it from every angle, since it is a three-dimensional work of art. When you are looking at a work of sculpture from a particular point of view, you might be the only person who has ever seen it from that exact point, because there are an infinite number of points from which to view such a work. When I photograph sculpture, I always photograph it from many different angles. I have even done two books on a single work of sculpture with a myriad of photographs showing what I have discovered with my camera eye.

Public relations is the same: We have to look at every angle, whether we are dealing with an issue, a company, an institution, or a government. We have to see it from the point of view of employees, management, the public, consumers, suppliers, and investors. In my opinion, that is the art of public relations. And I think the experience I have had in photographing sculpture for the many books I have published over the years is somehow related to the work I have done as a public relations practitioner for even more years.

The One True Measurement

There have been many attempts to measure the results of public relations statistically: analyzing media coverage, evaluating public attitudes, using public opinion polls, and so on. I have been in this business since 1948, and over the decades, many different approaches have been tried to determine the best way to measure the results of public relations in a formal and convincing way.

A number of methodologies have proved useful in specific situations, but my own feeling is that it is difficult to prove a cause and effect relationship in our business. To me, the true test of effectiveness is when a partnership exists with a client in which management knows intuitively that real value is being contributed. All the parties concerned know when it is working well.

Genuine Quality Brings a Campaign to Life

When there is a great story to tell, it is not difficult for outstanding results to be achieved. For instance, we are currently doing a lot of pro bono work with the United Nations, since Kofi Annan, the Secretary-General, happens to be longtime personal friend of mine. When he was elected Secretary-General, I told him we would do anything in our power to be helpful to him, and we have done many things together. One of our projects was to organize a millennium conference of religious and spiritual leaders at the U.N. We were able to get almost 2,000 spiritual leaders from around the world, from almost every conceivable religious tradition, to participate. They came to the U.N. for a two-and-a-half-day conference to discuss how they could be helpful in achieving peace in the new century. We had 40 or 50 members of our firm staff working on that project, and our whole company was thrilled to be involved with the U.N. at the highest level and to do something that was very satisfying and worthwhile. Of course, the press coverage around the world was extraordinary, and as a result of that gathering, plans are now under way for the creation of a Council of Religious and Spiritual Leaders to provide support wherever possible to the work of the U.N.

To give another very gratifying example, we are currently working with our client, Novartis, on a campaign for a new miracle drug that cures a certain form of cancer. It received the fastest approval by the FDA of any drug in history. We are developing a campaign featuring people who were at death's door whose lives were saved with this drug. The opportunity to work on such miracle stories is extraordinarily gratifying.

We use advertising as part of our campaign to get the message across, although we recognize that what a company says about itself or its products is different from what others say about the product. We try to find people who can tell the story about the product in their own way.

Advertising has a special role to play in such a campaign, but there are many other techniques to convey the message, and they are an integral part of the communications program.

We all know of great brands that have made their mark through sustained communications and marketing efforts – Coca-Cola being the number-one brand in the world today. We worked for many years for a company that is now known as Sara Lee. Before becoming Sara Lee, it was called Consolidated Foods Company, a name chosen by the founder, Nathan Cummings. One of his acquisitions was the Sara Lee Company, which was in the bakery business. When Nathan Cummings died, John Bryan, who was then the CEO, decided to change the name of the company. He realized the brand name "Sara Lee" had much more extensive recognition around the country than any other name he might choose, so he decided to adopt that as the name of the parent company. That well-known product brand has added substantial value to the visibility and public recognition of the whole company, and over the years this proved to be an extremely wise decision.

There is another story, in the world of art, rather than business, that I think is quite revealing. The sculptor Henry Moore was a good friend of mine, and I have published several books on his work, one of which was a description of my own personal relationship with him over the years. At one time, Kenneth Clark, the famous art historian, said that Moore was the most famous Englishman in the world, and some people suggested that since I am in the public relations business, I must have been responsible to some extent for Moore's fame. But I know that's ridiculous. Moore became well known because he was a great artist, not because of public relations. We shouldn't ever make the mistake of thinking that widespread public recognition might be achieved if it is not genuinely deserved.

I believe public relations can be part of the process in establishing brand recognition, but never the sole cause. Without genuine quality, all the promotion in the world will not create greatness, either in business or in art.

Ethics in Public Relations

We have long had an Ethics Committee at our firm, and when we are concerned about an ethical issue, we discuss it seriously with members of the Committee. We always have an outside advisor who is a paid consultant, as well as members of our staff, on our Committee. Over the years, we have had priests, rabbis, ministers, philosophers, and others as members of our Committee. And we have sometimes advised our clients to rethink their positions on certain critical issues because of discussions in our Ethics Committee. We have even resigned accounts when we have felt an ethical problem was involved.

The best advice we ever received from one of our ethics advisers is not to make quick or facile judgments when faced with a difficult issue. One experience I had in the early days of my career has served as a model for me. When Senator McCarthy was looking for communists under every rock, in every company and organization, there were a lot of people in the communications world who were called before his Senate Committee and asked if they had ever been communists. They could take the Fifth Amendment, which gave them the right not to answer that question without prejudice, and not to answer any other questions that followed. Many people who were called to testify took advantage of that constitutional right not to reveal anything that might be problematic in their lives, and also not to reveal anything about friends who might have come under investigation. Senator McCarthy called them Fifth Amendment communists – as far as he was concerned, if they pleaded the Fifth Amendment, they were as bad as if they had confessed to being communists. McCarthy pressured employers to fire anybody who pleaded the Fifth Amendment.

Since we believed in protecting constitutional rights, a number of public relations people who had been fired for pleading the Fifth Amendment came to us looking for jobs. One executive who had worked at a hospital in Denver pleaded the Fifth Amendment and had been fired; he applied for a job with us, and we hired him. Then a journalist who worked for *The New York Times* pleaded the

249

Fifth Amendment, and he was fired. He applied for a job with us, and we hired him, as well. We were a small company at the time, perhaps 25 or 30 people, so word soon got around that if you took the Fifth Amendment and got fired, go to Ruder Finn for a job. Soon a third man who took the Fifth Amendment applied for a job, and we began to worry about what we should do. Three of us were managing the company then, Bill Ruder and I together with Paul Zucker, who was our executive vice president. Paul said, "We cannot refuse to hire a man because he exercised his constitutional right. That doesn't make any sense." But Bill and I were worried that our firm might become a target of investigation if we hired too many people who had pleaded the Fifth Amendment. We went back and forth on this issue and finally asked Dr. Ernest Johnson, a professor of philosophy at Columbia University, if he could help. He said, "If you fellows will come to my office and spend a couple of hours, I'll help you think it through."

So the three of us went to Professor Johnson's office to talk about our problem. He said at the outset, "I'm not going to tell you what to do, but I'm going to help you analyze the ethical issues involved, and then you decide what you want to do. The way to examine the problem," he said, "is not to ask what is right or wrong, because in this instance, as in many others, there may be no simple right or wrong. What you have to do is think of the consequences of the different choices you might make. You may have two or three, or even as many as five choices, and you have to think of what will happen if you make any one of these choices, and then decide what consequences you think it would be wise to accept." As we talked, we realized if we continued our policy of respecting people's constitutional rights and continued to hire people who had pleaded the Fifth Amendment, at some point we would become visible to Senator McCarthy and his staff. We would ourselves become a target, and the whole company would suffer. So the question became: What would be the right number of Fifth Amendment pleaders to hire? We decided if we hired a third person, at our small-size company, it would begin to make us vulnerable. But then we came up with a new idea. If we approached other PR firms and persuaded them to hire qualified professionals who had pleaded the Fifth Amendment, just as we had done, we could help these people to get good jobs, and at the same time deflect any attention from ourselves as the only firm that was following that policy. We felt comfortable with that solution, and we did help get the man a job at another firm. We were able to do the same thing with others who had pleaded the Fifth Amendment and who came to us for a job. That was a good lesson on how to carefully examine an ethical dilemma and come to a resolution that is reliable and responsible. We have continued to examine ethical issues with the same care through our Ethics Committee ever since.

Be Careful About What You Wish For

We have an Executive Trainees program that is probably the oldest and still the largest in the field. We have three terms in the course of the year, and for each term some 15 to 20 college graduates come to us for about four months to learn about public relations and work on accounts. When they are through, we hire many of them to become members of our staff. Most of the interns have majored in English literature in college, although there are also others who majored in public relations, politics, or philosophy. But we have found their academic background is not especially important – what makes people successful in public relations is a capacity to be persistent and dogged in trying to achieve results. Very often you run into obstacles in the course of a public relations assignment, and only if you have the mental capacity to persist in trying to find solutions will you succeed.

When I address our trainees, I tell them a story about one of my own early experiences in public relations. We had a client who wanted to get a story about a new product published in *LIFE* magazine, which at that time was the major publication in the country. They were convinced that getting such a story would instantly make that product a success. We advised the client against that approach, explaining that it was most unlikely that one story would achieve such an objective. A successful public relations program would have to include a variety of well thought-out efforts on behalf of the product, rather than only one goal. But the client was insistent. It turned out to be a difficult assignment, and it took us a whole year to get that story in *LIFE* magazine. We encountered obstacles everywhere, but we never took "no" for an answer, and we found a way around every objection or problem we faced. We actually had to create a special project that justified *LIFE* doing the story. When it was finally published, the client was thrilled. But he discovered – as we had predicted – that one story does not guarantee success. He sat by his telephone after the story came out, waiting for orders for his product to pour in, but of course, they did not come. He had no marketing program in place and had mistakenly thought public relations alone was going to achieve his goal.

I tell that story to our trainees because it illustrates that first, you have to be persistent in carrying out your assignment; you cannot take no for an answer; you have to find a way somehow to achieve results for your client; and second, you have to have a realistic point of view about how to help your client achieve his or her real goal. Your supposed success may not do any good if a well-thought-out program and an effective follow-up is not part of your strategy.

Public Relations – A Profession?

The reputation of public relations has been discussed since I started in this business. "Public relations for public relations" has been called for again and again by many of our fellow practitioners – and for good reason. Critics have the impression that public relations is not a very serious activity, that it has to do with perceptions, not reality. Even my friend, Bill Safire, who started out in life as a public relations man, every now and then permits himself in one of his columns to talk about public relations people as "flacks." Others call us "spin doctors" who try to twist the truth. I bristle when I see such words in print or when people make disparaging comments about public relations.

I am on the board of directors of a company that has recently dealt with a crisis, and when I made a recommendation as to steps we might take to deal with the problem, one of my fellow board members, who is a lawyer, said "Oh, that's just public relations." I reminded him that public relations was not "fluff." It can be essential to the future of an enterprise. This negative reputation of public relations is something we have been struggling with for a long time.

The Public Relations Society of America has tried to deal with the problem by developing an accreditation program to establish public relations as a recognized profession. But I believe public relations is not really a profession. A profession has a long tradition of rules and regulations, like law, medicine, or education, where there is an established body of knowledge that is the foundation of the work to be done. In law, there are a judge, a jury, and a trial by which hopefully responsible judgments can be made. In public relations, there is no such body of knowledge, and we have no authority to make such judgments. If I want to persuade the public that our client is credible and should be supported, I have to realize I am talking to my friends and my family and not to a formal court of judgment. I do not want to persuade my friends about anything I do not believe in myself.

In public relations, we cannot be advocates for something we don't believe is right. The major challenge for us is to find a way to establish ourselves as an important and serious function, representing clients we personally support, but not make claims about professionalism that are unrealistic.

A lot of people have been trying to change the name of our business from "public relations" to something else. They talk about us as "communications counselors," "strategic marketing consultants," and so on. Unfortunately, I think we are stuck with the term "public relations." I do not think we will ever find another name for what we do. But one day somebody is going to figure out how to make those words become recognized as a serious, substantive function, and not a superficial one.

Realizing the Full Potential of PR

Public relations did not change much from 1948 to 1990. Then, with the computer revolution, everything became different. The changes that took place in public relations in the last ten years are far greater than the ones that took place over the previous 40 years. And I think there are more changes to come.

Public relations will become more systematic in the future, and we will have more ways of communicating and more ways of evaluating our success. We will have a more refined and sophisticated way of doing business. There will be more order in the work we do. Perhaps as that happens, we may ultimately be qualified as genuine professionals.

I hope that in the process of becoming more systematic, we will not lose our creativity and sensitivity. We need to be intellectually alert; we need to be culturally sensitive; we need to be responsive to societal needs; and we need to be conscious of ethical concerns. Only if we keep those values in mind, can public relations realize its full potential as an essential function in a democratic society.

David Finn has had an outstanding career that spans more than 50 years as a key executive in the field of public relations and as a widely published author. As co-founder, chairman, and CEO of Ruder·Finn, Inc., one of the largest independent public relations firms in the world, he has been a leader in exploring the ethical and philosophical dimensions of public relations, as well as in creating innovative approaches that have enhanced its effectiveness and broadened its contributions. He is also an accomplished photographer of sculpture, a painter, and a writer on art, with more than 70 books to his credit.

Clients of Ruder·Finn have included many Fortune 500 corporations as well as privately-held companies, trade associations, foreign governments and agencies, colleges and universities and not-for-profit organizations.

Mr. Finn has played a major role in the work the firm has done for international clients in France, Greece, Japan, Israel, Italy, New Zealand, Sweden, Switzerland, the United Kingdom, and other countries. He has been an advisor to the World Bank, and in the United States has been involved in programs for the White House, the United Nations and various government agencies including the Federal Reserve Board. He has written a periodic column for Roll Call, the newspaper of the Congress, and articles by him have been published in Forbes, Fortune, Harper's, the Saturday Review, the Harvard Business Review, the California Business Review, Across the Board, Management Review, and Reader's Digest. He produced a series of public service ads on "The Art of Leadership" for Forbes magazine.

Mr. Finn is a former chairman of the board of Cedar Crest College and a member of the board of directors of the Institute for the Future. He is on the board of the Academy of American Poets; The American Forum for Global Education; The New Hope Foundation; and MUSE Film and Television; and he is treasurer of the Business Committee for the Arts. He is a former editor-in-chief of Sculpture Review magazine.

Mr. Finn is a Fellow of the American Academy of Arts and Sciences and was appointed by President Clinton as a member of the Advisory Council for the National Endowment for the Humanities.

Mr. Finn is a graduate of The College of the City of New York.

ASPATORE MARKETING REVIEW
Tear Out This Page and Mail or Fax To:

Aspatore Books, PO Box 883, Bedford, MA 01730
Or Fax To (617) 249-1970

Name:

Email:

Shipping Address:

City: State: Zip:

Billing Address:

City: State: Zip:

Phone:

Lock in at the Current Rates Today-Rates Increase Every Year
Please Check the Desired Length Subscription:

1 Year ($1,090) _____   2 Years (Save 10%-$1,962) _____
5 Years (Save 20%-$4,360) _____   10 Years (Save 30%-$7,630) _____
Lifetime Subscription ($24,980) _____

(If mailing in a check you can skip this section but please read fine print below and sign below)
Credit Card Type (Visa & Mastercard & Amex):

Credit Card Number:

Expiration Date:

Signature:

Would you like us to automatically bill your credit card at the end of your subscription so there is no discontinuity in service? (You can still cancel your subscription at any point before the renewal date.) Please circle: Yes   No

*(Please note the billing address much match the address on file with your credit card company exactly)

Terms & Conditions

We shall send a confirmation receipt to your email address. If ordering from Massachusetts, please add 5% sales tax on the order (not including shipping and handling). If ordering from outside of the US, an additional $51.95 per year will be charged for shipping and handling costs. All issues are paperback and will be shipped as soon as they become available. Sorry, no returns or refunds at any point unless automatic billing is selected, at which point you may cancel at any time before your subscription is renewed (no funds shall be returned however for the period currently subscribed to). Issues that are not already published will be shipped upon publication date. Publication dates are subject to delay-please allow 1-2 weeks for delivery of first issue. If a new issue is not coming out for another month, the issue from the previous quarter will be sent for the first issue. For the most up to date information on publication dates and availability please visit www.Aspatore.com.

Everyone Is a Marketer, Media Matters, Technology and the Guerrilla Marketer, and Dollars and Sense. A must have for any big time marketing executive, small business owner, entrepreneur, marketer, advertiser, or any one interested in the amazing, proven power of guerrilla marketing.

Bigwig Briefs: HR & Building a Winning Team (ISBN: 1587620154)

Industry Experts Reveal the Secrets to Hiring, Retaining Employees, Fostering Teamwork, and Building Winning Teams of All Sizes
Bigwig Briefs: Human Resources & Building a Winning Team includes knowledge excerpts from some of the leading executives in the business world. These highly acclaimed executives explain the secrets behind hiring the best employees, incentivizing and retaining key employees, building teamwork, maintaining stability, encouraging innovation, and succeeding as a group.

Inside the Minds: Leading Women (ISBN: 1587620197)

What it Takes for Women to Succeed and Have it All in the 21st Century - *Inside the Minds: Leading Women* features CEOs and executives from companies such as Prudential, Women's Financial Network, SiliconSalley.com, Barclays Global Investors, RealEco.com, AgentArts, Kovair, MsMoney.com, LevelEdge and AudioBasket. These highly acclaimed women explain how to balance personal and professional lives, set goals, network, start a new company, learn the right skills for career advancement and more.

Inside the Minds: The Wireless Industry (ISBN: 1587620200)

Industry Leaders Discuss the Future of the Wireless Revolution - *Inside the Minds: The Wireless Industry* features leading CEOs from companies such as AT & T Wireless, Omnisky, Wildblue, AirPrime, Digital Wireless, Aperto Networks, Air2Web, LGC Wireless, Arraycomm, Informio and Extenta. Items discussed include the future of the wireless industry, wireless devices, killer-apps in the wireless industry, the international landscape, government issues and more.

Inside the Minds: Venture Capitalists (ISBN: 1587620014)

Inside the High Stakes and Fast Paced World of Venture Capital - *Inside the Minds: Venture Capitalists* features leading partners from Softbank, ICG, Sequoia Capital, CMGI, New Enterprise Associates, Bertelsmann Ventures, TA Associates, Kestrel Venture Management, Blue Rock Capital, Novak Biddle Venture Partners, Mid-Atlantic Venture Funds, Safeguard Scientific, Divine interVentures, and Boston Capital Ventures. Learn how some of the best minds behind the Internet revolution value companies, assess business models, and identify opportunities in the marketplace.

Inside the Minds: Leading Consultants (ISBN: 1587620596)

Industry Leaders Share Their Knowledge on the Future of the Consulting Profession and Industry - *Inside the Minds: Leading Consultants* features leading CEOs/Managing Partners from some of the world's largest consulting companies. These industry leaders share their knowledge on the future of the consulting industry, being an effective team player, the everlasting effects of the Internet and technology, compensation, managing client relationships, motivating others, teamwork, the future of the consulting profession and other important topics.

Inside the Minds: Leading CEOs (ISBN: 1587620553)
Industry Leaders Share Their Knowledge on Management, Motivating Others, and Profiting in Any Economy - *Inside the Minds: Leading CEOs* features some of the biggest name, proven CEOs in the world. These highly acclaimed CEOs share their knowledge on management, the Internet and technology, client relationships, compensation, motivating others, building and sustaining a profitable business in any economy and making a difference at any level within an organization.

Inside the Minds: Internet Bigwigs (ISBN: 1587620103)
Industry Experts Forecast the Future of the Internet Economy (After the Shakedown) - *Inside the Minds: Internet Bigwigs* features a handful of the leading minds of the Internet and technology revolution. These individuals include executives from Excite (Founder), Beenz.com (CEO), Organic (CEO), Agency.com (Founder), Egghead (CEO), Credite Suisse First Boston (Internet Analyst), CIBC (Internet Analyst) and Sandbox.com. Items discussed include killer-apps for the 21st century, the stock market, emerging industries, international opportunities, and a plethora of other issues affecting anyone with a "vested interest" in the Internet and technology revolution.

Bigwig Briefs: Management & Leadership (ISBN: 1587620146)
Industry Experts Reveal the Secrets How to Get There, Stay There, and Empower Others That Work For You
Bigwig Briefs: Management & Leadership includes knowledge excerpts from some of the leading executives in the business world. These highly acclaimed executives explain how to break into higher ranks of management, how to become invaluable to your company, and how to empower your team to perform to their utmost potential.

Bigwig Briefs: The Golden Rules of the Internet Economy (After the Shakedown) (ISBN: 1587620138)
Industry Experts Reveal the Most Important Concepts From the First Phase of the Internet Economy
Bigwig Briefs: The Golden Rules of the Internet Economy includes knowledge excerpts from some of the leading business executives in the Internet and Technology industries. These highly acclaimed executives explain where the future of the Internet economy is heading, mistakes to avoid for companies of all sizes, and the keys to long term success.

Bigwig Briefs: Start-ups Keys to Success (ISBN: 1587620170)
Industry Experts Reveal the Secrets to Launching a Successful New Venture
Bigwig Briefs: Start-ups Keys to Success includes knowledge excerpts from some of the leading VCs, CEOs CFOs, CTOs and business executives in every industry. These highly acclaimed executives explain the secrets behind the financial, marketing, business development, legal, and technical aspects of starting a new venture.

Bigwig Briefs: The Art of Deal Making (ISBN: 1587621002)
Leading Deal Makers Reveal the Secrets to Negotiating, Leveraging Your Position and Inking Deals - *Bigwig Briefs: The Art of Deal Making* includes knowledge excerpts from some of the biggest name CEOs, Lawyers, VPs of BizDev and Investment Bankers in the world on ways to master the art of deal making. These highly acclaimed deal makers from companies such as Prudential, Credite Suisse First Boston, Barclays, Hogan & Hartson, Proskaur Rose, AT&T and others explain the secrets behind keeping your deal skills sharp, negotiations, working with your team, meetings schedules and environment, deal parameters and other important topics.

Other Best Selling Business Books Include:

Inside the Minds: Leading Accountants
Inside the Minds: Leading CTOs
Inside the Minds: Leading Deal Makers
Inside the Minds: Leading Wall St. Investors
Inside the Minds: Leading Investment Bankers
Inside the Minds: Internet BizDev
Inside the Minds: Internet CFOs
Inside the Minds: Internet Lawyers
Inside the Minds: The New Health Care Industry
Inside the Minds: The Financial Services Industry
Inside the Minds: The Media Industry
Inside the Minds: The Real Estate Industry
Inside the Minds: The Automotive Industry
Inside the Minds: The Telecommunications Industry
Inside the Minds: The Semiconductor Industry
Bigwig Briefs: Term Sheets & Valuations
Bigwig Briefs: Venture Capital
Bigwig Briefs: Become a CEO
Bigwig Briefs: Become a CTO
Bigwig Briefs: Become a VP of BizDev
Bigwig Briefs: Become a CFO
Bigwig Briefs: Small Business Internet Advisor
Bigwig Briefs: Human Resources & Building a Winning Team
Bigwig Briefs: Career Options for Law School Students
Bigwig Briefs: Career Options for MBAs
Bigwig Briefs: Online Advertising
OneHourWiz: Becoming a Techie
OneHourWiz: Stock Options
OneHourWiz: Public Speaking
OneHourWiz: Making Your First Million
OneHourWiz: Internet Freelancing
OneHourWiz: Personal PR & Making a Name For Yourself
OneHourWiz: Landing Your First Job
OneHourWiz: Internet & Technology Careers (After the Shakedown)

Go to www.Aspatore.com for a
Complete List of Titles!